MESSAGES OF HOPE

BY

JONATHON MCCLELLAN

MESSAGES

OF HOPE

JONATHON MCCLELLAN

TEXAS BOOK PUBLISHERS' ASSOCIATION

HOUSTON TEXAS

Dedication

For my beloved parents. Everything that you have struggled so hard for was not in vain, because your countless sacrifices and faithfulness to God is like a golden medallion that I wear around my neck always reminding me of the way I should go.

To Shaquan, Katie, and Maria. Without your friendship, I would have given up long ago.

And for my partner, love, and dearest companion Paul. In every way, you have made me a better man and your love is more powerful than the tidal force the moon creates in gentle seas.

Contents

Preface

"…we also glory in our sufferings, because
we know that suffering produces perseverance;
perseverance, character; and character, hope."
(Romans 5:3-4 NIV).

Beauty for Ashes

Pain was essential to my life. I was birthed through pain. It was my mother's sacrifice which yielded fruit. Without loss there is no life, but what is lost? Certainly, her own body became my vessel; this revealed that the seed of life was inside of her: life inside life. When I was born, I was a life in a life still within the biosphere known as Earth. I am composed of the materials found in Earth. When I drink water, I observe rivers in myself. Dirty water in turn pollutes me, so when I hurt the source, I hurt myself. That is not to say that water is my source, but that all life which is connected to water or all life which is in relationship to water is connected.

All pain flows through your river for we all drink from the same source. Do not reject the water because it has pain in it. You need the pain to grow. It will nourish you with wisdom, patience, endurance, a greater appreciation for love, and understanding all the more. These words will not be simple, but everything has a purpose. Without bitterness, would I know sweetness? Without sorrow, would I know joy? Without darkness, would I know light? I know this: that I am who I am not just because of the good experiences, but because of the bad ones also.

When I jumped in the water it was cold, but I learned how to swim. Soon my body adjusted, and the water did not seem cold any longer. It was not the water that changed, but I. The discomfort that I experienced from the cold water was the bridge to swimming. The cold then, was not my enemy, but the door. Likewise, pain is not the enemy, but the doorway to life fully experienced.

Prayer

Please God, make me wiser. Help me not to resent the pain, but to give thanks in all things with a genuine heartfelt appreciation. Heal my heart Lord and take the sorrow, anger, regret, hatred, bitterness, and all manner of sickness. Turn my weeping into shouts of joy. Let me say, "The Lord has given me beauty for my ashes".

Amen.

"Be still, and know that I am God." (Psalm 46:10 ESV)

Silent Prayer

"Lord, hear our prayer."

It is not words which move You. Beautiful sayings and eloquent speech do not persuade You. I am reminded that You look at the heart and weigh it in Your hand. Words won't call my Father down, but my heart causes You to stoop down. There are words that my heart cannot say to anyone else, but You. For You understand the heart and You speak its language.

My prayer cannot be put into words. It is with my heart then that I pray, for You listen to my heart. I will be silent and let my heart speak. By intention I call to You. By my will I open my heart to You. You shall hear what lays heavily on my heart. You will know my pain and my joy. There are no secret places in my heart; everything is open. What I have wanted to say for so long, I can finally say in deep feelings.

What is a prayer Lord? Is it not communication with You? Surely, You listen to my heart all day long. Surely, You know the song that it plays. Let me escape words and journey somewhere beyond articulation. Let my heart be a feast of love. May deep wells flow from within. I welcome You in. Communication without words. All I have to do is feel what I feel.

Prayer

Lord, teach me to listen. Quietly You whisper, "I love you," all day long. If only I knew how to listen. Let me hear Your heart Lord. I will not listen with my ears, for you are not listening to my heart with ears. I will hear the sound of Your voice guiding me to love. When love is present, You are near. You are love. I shall rest in Your love. You are ever present and listening. I must be silent if I am to listen. In my heart there is a silent prayer which must be made. Thank You Lord, for teaching me that I can pray silently and for being the One who listens.

Amen.

Keep Hoping

It was because of hope that I first found God. In my darkest days, when my strength had left me and everything that I had relied upon was no longer enough, hope delivered me. Hope brought me out of my comfort zone into a search for a guarantee that everything was going to be alright. That guarantee could only be an answer from God. I had so many questions…so many insecurities. The world was constantly changing and at a pace so fast that it left me feeling uncertain, afraid, and troubled. It was because I hoped that God loved me that I searched for and discovered a greater love than I could ever imagine. Hope in God and hope in His love, because one hardly finds a treasure without first hoping that it exists.

How could you endure winter if you did not hope for spring? How could you cross the ocean if you did not hope that land would be on the other side? Or how could you gain a harvest if you did not hope for rain when you planted the seeds? It is often that we hope in what we do not know, but it is because we hope that we seek and do find. Some might call you crazy because of your hope, and some may leave you because your hope offends them, but in the end, you will be called wise and they the fools. The wise gain for themselves joy in abundance, but fools gain only regret. Do not leave this world regretting what you could have had if only you had not given up hope but leave satisfied.

What one hopes in, there will their treasure be. Therefore, hope in what can give you a future and not in the world, for the world is temporary. God is eternal and so is His love. He teaches wisdom and discretion. The love of God will protect you from harm and keep your loved ones in safety. Having a relationship with God is priceless and cannot be compared with anything the world offers, for nothing in the world is like Him. Because I hoped in God, I found peace, love, and joy. More importantly, I found a friend.

Prayer

Blessed Father,

Do not let our hopes die. Keep us from hoping in the wrong things. Bless You for Your wisdom and understanding. You give us hope. Give us the strength to keep hoping and fulfil our hopes quickly. Thank You God for every-thing that You are and have granted us.

Amen.

"Be completely humble and gentle; be patient, bearing with one another in love. Make every effort to keep the unity of the Spirit through the bond of peace." (Ephesians 4:2-3 NIV)

Life or Death

Where there is love, there is life, and, where there is hate, there is death. Between love and hate, there are a range of feelings such as like and dislike. It is possible to dislike someone, but love them; and to like someone, but hate them. We are complex creatures with complex emotions. Apathy is rare, but when it is present... is out of sight and out of mind. As humans, we will feel a range of emotions in our lifetime. Our feelings do not define us, but rather, what we do with our emotions leave behind our legacy and memory to the ones who will come after us.

One does not blame a child for committing a crime that they do not understand. Therefore, understanding is more important than intention. Jesus asked His Father to forgive those who knowingly crucified Him because they lacked understanding. The reason why so many people disagree with each other is because there exists a multitude of varied understanding. If someone does not understand something as you do, then they likely do not feel the same way you do either. Reason is not void of emotion, for all principles require some passion to exist. How one feels about what is right and what is wrong determines the action taken far more often than one's understanding. Many people understand right and wrong, and yet… have not come together in agreement because they are different.

If a woman loves her unborn child, then he or she is already alive to her. However, a woman who does not want her unborn child, may not feel the same way. It is possible to neither hate nor love the unborn and have varying conclusions on when life begins to matter. When life matters, it starts in the heart. God fell in love with us, which is the reason why we were ever born. Love gives birth to life as it does children. When someone does not understand your position, remember, where there is love, there is life. It is possible to disagree with someone without condemning them. Every emotion has a consequence, and every action is forever written in the past. Therefore, consider what you want to leave behind. You can make this world better for everyone with your love.

Prayer

Father God,

Teach us to love one another despite our differences. Help us to love even when it is not convenient. We often want to understand, but rarely each other. Bring us together in love. By Your Spirit Lord we pray,

Amen.

The Search for Truth

My perception is one society has deemed to be inherently flawed. I was diagnosed as having Schizophrenia, Psychosis, ADHD, Oppositional Defiance, and Bi-polar disorder; characterized as not being able to differentiate between fact and fiction, a mood disorder, and psychotic. Some people call me crazy, I kind of like this really because the best ones are. I would say that someone else's defining of me amputates from a much larger understanding of who I really am. Thus, I would say that I am misunderstood.

As an outcast, I have learned that the difference between fact and fiction is what some people describe as trust while for others it is faith. Science does not prove anything but gives us reasons why we believe what we believe. We believe that there are other galaxies out there because technology gives us reasons: telescopes capture images from light years away. I have never been to another galaxy, however, and my belief that they exist comes from my trust of another's report. I have faith, but I do not know anything. This is because of a humility that comes from observing history. Many people believed that the Earth was flat until they sailed around it. Pluto was a planet until they noticed that it was a dwarf planet. Whether you are a Schizophrenic or not, differentiating between fact and fiction can be a struggle to some degree. Our definitions, concepts, and points of view change over time. What we know now, in the future, may in fact be described as what we thought we knew.

Knowing what something is, is not the same as knowing why something is, and for every front there is a back. Even if you did know what was behind every door, knew all the secrets of the cosmos, and nothing were hidden from you I have learned, as Paul the Apostle suggests, that if you do not have love it all amounts to nothing. That is the beauty of my end of the dinner table. As I walk through life, I know less and less.

In my story I am the observer. As an observer I play a role: I interpret. Or in other words, I create. My view at the dinner table tells a story of its own. I cannot observe reality because each seat at the table possesses a point of view that I do not. The observer takes the elements of reality and assigns an identity. He might describe the element wind as cold or nature as beautiful. At another seat, however, the observer might describe the elements differently. One may be cold while another is hot. Reality is neither cold nor hot because reality is formless. Only the observer describes the elements making up our universe. Without the observer there is no beauty, evil, or imperfection for who would describe its character?

If there is no one to observe that a comet is hurling through space does that mean that is does not? Who is to say? Without anyone to describe the comet there is no reaction; that is to say there is no interpretation. What was the comet before anyone ever described it? Formless; otherwise, who differentiated between the comet and outer space? Without the "who" there is no "what". I suppose then that reality is the side-effect of observation. Since childhood I have created a world: an interpretation. It has gotten me into a lot of trouble, but it has also gotten me into a great deal of fun.

The problem is that I am mentally ill. My observation cannot be relied upon because I do not see things the way they are. I am cold while everyone else is hot. If I hear spirits and no one else does, then I am crazy. My observation contains madness. Perhaps in the future we will not validate an observation based on whether or not everyone agrees about it but validate that the observation is our creation. Everyone is free to create, interpret, and tell his or her own story without being labeled and marginalized.

If reality is our own observation, then what is truth? I have struggled with this question for years. When I see demons, but the doctors see a psychotic break I wonder who is seeing the truth. I prayed for the answer and spent years pondering whether or not I was living an illusion. It was agony because at times I really thought that I was crazy. Not being able to rely on my own senses left me in a state of constant confusion and fear. I became obsessed with knowing whether or not I was seeing things as they were.

The quest for truth has always been my life's pursuit, but it was made harder by the persistent voice of my critic. I was drowning in a sea of many voices, and all of them were saying the same thing, "You are out of your mind". A silent torture griped my mind and life lost its taste, until I arrived at this conclusion: one does not have to know everything in order to enjoy life.

Prayer

"They will neither hunger nor thirst, nor will the desert heat or the sun beat down on them. He who has compassion on them will guide them and lead them beside springs of water."--Isaiah 49:10

Lord, When I am shaken, You are not. When I am afriad, You are my rock. When I am unloved, You are love. When I am despised, You are compassiate. When I am tired and weary, You are my rest. When I'm lost in despair, You are my guiding sherpard.

Father, I need compassion from others. I need compassion for myself too. Help me notice and embrace compassion offered to me. Help me extend compassion to myself and others, especially when it's hard to do.

Amen.

Understanding

If humanity is to come together, then it will be with the effort of humble people who try to understand one another. When you try to understand others, those same people will try to understand you. Most friendships that last happens because of the effort that was put into the relationships. Whatever you give is what you eventually get back. Someone who seeks to understand you is that much more likely to get your understanding than someone who shows little interest in your thoughts and feelings. The many who spend their lifetime trying to be understood often never get anywhere because if everyone is speaking at the same time, then there is no one listening.

Wanting to be understood is not bad, but if your happiness depends on another's approval, then what will you do when they criticize you? There are great people who are never understood in their own lifetime, and after they are re-discovered by the next generation, are spoken very highly of. The more you are able to understand others, the more you'll be able to speak to your generation. Being understanding is not about what you know as much as it is about your attitude. By listening often, you show that you value others and teach others to do the same.

It is extremely lonely when no one around you understands you, but it is not something you can force. If you never listen to others, then who will listen to you? Listening is not just about being silent; listening in making an effort to see what the other person is seeing. It does not mean that you must always agree or never have something to say. Instead, show that you care. This may mean that you have to wait a while to be understood, but don't give up hoping that you will be one day. You may find only one person who truly understands you and you'll be doing better than some really great people who never found anyone who was able to. Always remember, God understands you, and you never have to go far to find Him.

Prayer

All knowing One,

You are not understood by many, and yet, You love us. Help us to be as patient. When we are overlooked and criticized falsely, please remind us of our own worth. Bless You Spirit, because You know who we are. May we feel the love You have for us, and may we be at peace within ourselves. Bless You Jesus, the One who knows what it means to be misunderstood.

Amen.

"May the Lord make your love increase and overflow for each other and for everyone else, just as ours does for you." (1 Thessalonians 3:12 NIV)

The Gift

Love has always been many gifts, but what is a gift that is not given? Unless the gift is given it can never become what it was meant to be. One does not smile from the inside, but it stretches across the lips from cheek to cheek for all to see. When we smile at others, we give a gift that comes from the heart. Then, once that gift is received by another, her love grows and responds with a smile of her very own. She will have then learned to smile, and not only that, but will find someone new to give her smile to.

Today, there are many smiles all around the world because God first smiled at us. God created us because He wanted someone to give His love to; He wanted to show His smile to His creation. The love of God gives life, otherwise, why would He have ever given the gift? Love hurts sometimes, and we all hurt sometimes. A baby cries when she wants to be held. Once the baby is in the arms of her mother, however, she stops crying because she craved love. As the baby lives off of the mother's milk, so too does she need love from the one who created her.

Milk is for the body, but love, is for the spirit. Jesus said, "Man shall not live off of bread alone, but by every word that proceeds out of the mouth of God." The "word" that Jesus spoke of is, in essence, the love of God. Without love, God words would be soundless, unheard, and of no effect. If God made mankind because He wanted to give us a gift, then we, by nature, were meant to receive that gift. My Earthly father taught me that love is not love unless it is given because love has always been, and always will be, an expression of the heart.

Prayer

Bless You Lord for Your precious love. You smiled at us, and now, we smile too. Protect these hearts that learned how to smile so that we, in kind, can give it back. Thank You for showing us the way. You have so much love for us, but it is not always understood. Help us to understand Your great love towards us. Show us how to love others as You have loved us.

Amen.

Beauty and the Bite

I stepped out for a breath of fresh air to enjoy the peaceful serenity of the dusk. As I'm sitting on the porch outside my house, I start to notice many mosquitoes flying around me. In a moment, I will be covered in little bites which on my skin become itchy red bumps, but I risk it. If I am to step out into the world, then I may be bitten. Soon, it doesn't matter anymore because as soon as I look up, I'm immediately captured by a vision so pure that I become transfixed in it.

The sun and the moon are sharing the sky in opposite positions: the sun setting in the west and the moon rising in the east. Clouds are covering the moon. As I look around, I start to notice the many dragonflies flying over my head. Birds beside me are resting on the treetops. The leaves, grass, and vines cover the Earth in green skin. The arms, legs, and feet are green. The hair is a sea of blues and yellows. Tree trunks resemble wise sages who have learned how to simply be.

As if keeping a promise, the itching from the mosquito bites tear at my serenity. My ankles are red, and my nails begin to bring salvation to the itching. Why did I come out here? It wasn't for the mosquitoes. This dance is but a metaphor for life: the beauty and the bite. Sometimes, life bites you, but it's worth it. Despite the mosquitoes, this was a good way to spend my evening.

Prayer

Hear me Lord. You have showed me that there will be times when I'm not enjoying my experience. Nevertheless, a baby is not born unless the mother suffers for it. New flowers do not spring up unless old flowers die and leave their seeds behind. One cannot swim in the ocean without feeling the cold. Dear Lord, teach us to dance. Show me that living is worth the pain that comes with it. What could I ever see if I never left my home? Sure, there was discomfort from the itching, but my heart is jumping for joy over the vision… over the experience.

Amen.

Consequences of Nature

If love hurts, then it is love. Ancient scriptures teach us that love hates evil. This means that if one pursues love, then they will inevitably pursue hate at the same time. If you love something, then you will hate what opposes it. One who values kindness will hate cruelty. Compassion opposes mercilessness. The truth is that we hate what hurts us. A lie can hurt, so we often hate lies. We learn to hate what hurts us because we love something else, say the truth. It is what we love which determines what we hate and vice-versa. As observed by Einstein: actions result in equal and opposite reactions. When we enjoy something more, something else is preferred less. As a result, love hurts and hurt people hate.

We are meant to love and must accept the pain that comes with love. Opposition is natural and is a result of being a creature with choices. One chooses what they love and what they hate. It is the gift of God to have choices, and the pain that comes with it is a necessary part of life. There are occasions in all of our lives where we are slaves to our hearts. When one loves another, they cannot always control it. This means that love is going to hurt as well without one's consent.

Struggle is a part of every relationship, but so too is growth. Wisdom is gained from lessons learned from pain. Everything is connected somehow. Joy is greatly valued when there was once sorrow. To make the distinction of good is to also discern what is evil. We need to remember that healthy hearts hurt sometimes.

When one is hurting in an area of their life: a relationship, sudden death, or tragedy, it means that they really enjoyed the time that they had. To be bitter is to have appreciated life in some other area.

Prayer

Heal our hearts Lord. Let suffering end and joy be everlasting. Abba, if I must endure pain, then lift me up when I fall. Having a choice to love or hate is a gift and a burden. Carry my burdens Lord. Jesus lead my heart, for I cannot always control what choices my heart makes. Teach me why love is sweet, and hatred is bitter. Lastly, reside in my heart Jesus and protect it.

Amen.

"Do not be overcome by evil, but overcome evil with good." (Romans 12:21 NIV)

A Love that Never Runs Out

Oh, how lovely it is to give love. When I give love, it is like the walls of a dam burst open. I realize, that as the waters travel freely, I am able to give even more love than before. The heart is a muscle like any other, and the more it is exercised, the stronger it becomes. Here's the magic of giving love: eventually, and sometimes immediately, you get it back. Love is not something you put in a jar and leave in your pantry, but it is given like a meal. That meal can feed five, five hundred, or five million, and like any meal, it gives strength to the one who eats it. This strength is actually a capacity for giving more love. So, as you give love, you create even more love, in yourself and others.

Love teaches love, kindness teaches kindness, and mercy teaches mercy. Without knowing it, by giving a kind word, we are leaving something behind for the next generation. Look for every opportunity then, to love, for love turns this world into a paradise. If love teaches love, then hate teaches hate, cruelty teaches cruelty, and apathy teaches apathy. We must then overcome hate with love. Without wood a fire goes out. If we do not feed our neighbors hate, then there will be less hate. The same is true of love.

There are a lot of fires in the world burning our people with a contagious hatred. We are surrounded on all sides by this flame. Our choices will either save this world or hasten its destruction.

God's people must be determined, dedicated, and diligent if we are to break the dams surrounding our hearts and cause love to flow like a mighty river. Overcome hate with love. Do not return hate for hate, but forgive, show mercy, and compassion. Then, you will have understanding. Love will lighten your heavy heart and change your enemy into a friend.

Prayer

Loving and merciful Spirit,

You have given us the most precious gift of love. Let us not bury it within ourselves. Help us to be vulnerable, and if we are injured for the sake of love, heal our hearts. Open our eyes to see the countless opportunities You have given us to love, and may we get it back a hundred-fold. Bless You Great Spirit for all that we shall receive.

Amen.

The Light of Hope

The Light of Hope is inside of you. As Gautama Buddha suggests, with your candle you can light a thousand other candles. Our light is powerful! Even if the whole world is covered in darkness and you open the curtain of a well-lit room wide open, no darkness will pour in. How great is our light if it comes from God!? I cannot fathom an answer.

However, I have noticed that if a room is dark and you open a curtain just a little to let the light in, the whole room fills with light. If God is the candle giving light to the rooms in our hearts, then we who are one in Christ have been made like Him.

Never forget that greater is He that is in you than he that is in the world (1 John 4:4).

You are the light the world needs. One person who realizes that God is inside of them can be the flame to a million souls who have never been told that they are special. There is more to the light than glamour; the light is a reflection of the love in our hearts. God is light just as He is love. His children are the same.

We are the answer to the peoples cry because you do not put a candle under a basket on the floor, but you set it on a candlestick high and it gives light to the whole house (Matthew 5:15).

There are five things that you need to remember:
1) You do not need to become what you already are.
2) You are someone who shines with a divine light.
3) You have the smile that someone has been waiting all day to see.
4) You are the gift God gave us.
5) You are light.

Prayer

Loving God,

I want to be a candle that You use to light other candles. Let Your love spread like wild-fires. People all over the world have something to say about the light, but Your son, Jesus, went beyond optical observation when He told us that we are gods. What do I do now Lord that I see that I am the light? What is my purpose? The Lord did not give me just one; because once it was completed my life would be over. Instead, You provided me with many ways and opportunities to light a candle. Let's start a fire Lord in the hearts of the people. Thank You, Lord, for these many gifts.

Amen.

Love at No Cost

The secret to how to love yourself is simply this: stop looking for a reason to love yourself because if you need a reason to love, then it is not love. If love has a cost, then its value has been measured. When the value of love is measured, it is forever limited by that measurement. Unless love is free, no one can afford it, for it is too great a gift to ever sell. Love is far greater than gold, so then, what commodity could we trade that would be of equal or of a greater value than love? There is altogether nothing as precious as love, for it is because of love that anything that ever was came to be.

By love, God created every living thing. He never required payment for our lives, rather, our life was His gift to us. If God did require payment, then the charge would exceed our lives; for as long as we kept on living, we would owe payment. Therefore, parents do not make their children debtors. On the contrary, because love is free, a good parent will keep giving their children love as long as they are alive. When love is a free gift, there is an endless supply. Do not measure love by requirements of beauty, wealth, or possessions because once they are gone the love runs out.

Love that is free is both given and received freely, which means that anyone who wants it should have it. If we are prejudiced, then we are not loving. We have heard it been said that, "if you do not love yourself, then no one else will." Consider this, if you do not love others, then how can you love yourself? The truth is that you cannot, because love's only standard is that it must and can only be for everyone. Otherwise, you have measured love and have made it altogether worthless. If God loves you freely, then you ought to love others and yourself at the same cost.

Prayer

Loving Father,

Bless You for Your great love. Teach us to love others and ourselves as You have loved us. Let us not be wise in our own eyes, but humble, meek, and tender. Undo our philosophies and grant us real wisdom. Do not let us fall into the ways of the world but teach us the ways of heaven. We need Your love so that we may know what it is and how to give it freely. Bless You heavenly Father, for we live because of Your love.

Amen.

Unanswered Questions

As our vision of the universe gets larger, our knowledge about it, gets smaller and smaller. Einstein observed that the more he learned, the less he knew. It is often that when we answer a question, ten new questions arise each leading us to more undiscovered and unanswered questions. I find that a flower is not just a stem and its petals, but it is also its seed. What is a seed without its journey? The flower is connected to generations of flowers. A person's name can imply where they come from and who they are connected to. A rock is the culmination of many smaller particles. I have found no simple answers, but always, more to discover.

Humility is considering the possibility that what we do not know what we do not know. I do not see all the pieces of life's puzzle or things that I have yet to experience. If I were to try to define anything, then that would mean pretending I had an understanding of universal truths when I do not fully comprehend anything. We believe that God exists, but what or rather who is God? I could say that God is love, but consider how long it would it take me to describe all of God's love if I could?

Why do so many religious people believe that God is love, but then, condemn people for not believing that their religion is the right one? They have neither learned what love is nor who God is, yet they can judge. How can we judge God's creation without knowing all the facts? Humanity has more in common than it realizes, for many faiths teach that God is love. The scriptures teach us that we have the ability to set aside our differences and be kind to one another. One day, differing faiths may have less strangers, and more friends. Perhaps, because if we know less, then there is more to learn about each other.

Prayer

Lord of mercy,

Only You know everything and only You can judge. Help us to be forgiving and kind to strangers. Grant us a humble spirit. Show us how to disagree lovingly. Bless You because You are patient with us. We love You, yet we do not know You fully. Help us to love those that we do know, yet don't comprehend.

Amen.

"After this I looked, and there before me was a great multitude that no one could count, from every nation, tribe, people and language, standing before the throne and before the Lamb. They were wearing white robes and were holding palm branches in their hands." (Revelation 7:9 NIV)

We Are One

O child of God, thou art a Jew, a Gentile, a Muslim, a Christian, a Hindu, a Buddhist, a stranger across the stars, and those not named. Who has positioned themselves to judge who is or is not a child of God? Can one judge another man's heart? You may not look like me, talk like me, or think like me, but it was God who made you unique; what is that to me? Who excluded you? It was not God. Was it not man? Today, He has called you His. We are all beloved children of God.

Why is it so natural to exclude others from the kingdom of God? I have never met anyone who has read the Lamb's Book of Life or knows the names written therein. Maybe God does not want us to judge who is worthy of heaven, less the tears measure the wheat. It was the religious authority who said to believe what they believed, and by the merits of their understanding did they undermine the gospel of grace. For it is not by theology or doctrine that is one justified, but the love of God justifies.

How can they who have not the love of God justify or condemn? Ask God yourselves. He will confirm you. The love of Jesus sought out the sinner. He did not condemn them but hung on a cross so that all might be included. Why did Jesus offer the Samaritan woman water even though she was not a Jew? He displayed the love of God which is not prejudiced.

Prayer

Lord,

If Jesus was not a Christian, then why do others have to be? Help those who doubt Your love for them. Let this divided house come together as one divine family. I am excluded by others because of my beliefs. Let Your love relieve the wounds caused by the continual rejection of my brothers and sisters. As Jesus said, "Forgive them, for they know not what they do." It is my desire Lord that Your people come together as one. I pray You bless this prayer and all who read it.

Amen.

Right or Righteous?

It is more important to be righteous than it is being right. If you do not have love, then you have gained nothing by being right. Words with malice, judgment, and manipulation in them defeat the purpose of being right. Some people look at the surface and judge incorrectly, so isn't it great that God never asked us to judge? You can be right, but that doesn't always mean it is time to be right. Sometimes being righteous means being patient, kind with your words, and sincere.

If I'm right, what does it gain me if my sister is harmed? Today, people have a hard time coming together if they don't always agree. Isn't it more righteous to agree to disagree in spirit, not just in word, by coming together to the same table? I'd rather not know anything. Consider me a fool. They call me an idealist, but I ask, "Do I have to be of a certain religion to feed the hungry?" No one I ever helped ever refused me because of my sexual orientation, the color of my skin, or any of my personal beliefs. A man dying of hunger will rarely refuse a meal. Should we make requirements of those who want to give?

There is something truly beautiful in coming together. I want to forget about who is right and who is wrong and laugh over the silliness of it all. How did things get so away from us? We are so divided now. If we don't do something, the next war will be here. Some would say it already is. Being righteous is forgiving when it is hard, when you know you are right, and when he or she is your enemy. Invite your enemy to your table.

You are the gift the world needs. The love has to start somewhere, and it is with you.

Prayer

Lord,

Show me a table where a Christian and a
Muslim sit together. On another end, let there
be an atheist next to a Rabbi, a harlot next to a
saint, a monk next to an assassin, and an Israeli
next to a Palestinian. Let there be peace in our
homes, so that when we leave, we can go in that
peace with the hopes that it will spread to others.
There is so little love for the stranger all because
we don't know who she is. Let the walls to our
hearts come down and the doors swing open.

Amen.

My First Bicycle

For many people around the world, turning seven is not usually the birthday that one reminisces about, but then...I could never forget my family at the Faith Mission homeless shelter and what they did for me that day. According to the National Center on Family Homelessness, about two and a half million children are homeless each year in America added into UNICEF's reporting of twenty-eight million children worldwide. At any given moment in America, out of a random group of thirty children, perhaps in a school or in a park, one of them will not know the safety and refuge of a good home. For some children it is because they lack parents who can care for them, for some it is due to poverty, and for others it is because being homeless is the safer alternative from being in the home.

There are so many homeless youths, but ironically, we hear so few of their voices. There is a misconception that just because we are living in the wealthiest nation on the planet such stories are impossible here. Poverty, however, is not limited by borders and emotional poverty can touch even the wealthiest of us. I was a lucky boy, and even more than that, blessed to have encountered so many heroes of the helpless when I was but six years old. My mother was pregnant at the time and she, my eighteen-month-old sister, and I were escaping the drug induced violent rages of my stepfather. In the middle of the night, out of desperation and fear of losing her unborn baby, my mother called the police, and we fled from our home. Even though that meant that we had become homeless overnight, it was better than having an enemy in the house.

That early August evening in the year 1995, the officer drove us to the YMCA homeless shelter in Fort Wane, Indiana and there we stayed for two short days before being transferred to Faith Mission in the nearby city of Elkhart. At first, I did not know what was going on or what the future would hold for us. I was happy to be away from my stepfather and overjoyed that my mother was finally safe. When you are a child, a mother's presence is more constant and important than the sun's; as long as I had her, no matter where we were, I felt safe. Faith Mission provided every convenience to make us feel comfortable. Due to my mother's condition, they turned the basement of their shelter into the likes of a new loft. Even though they were filled to capacity when we had arrived, they made room for us out of nothing.

Faith Mission lived up to the name, for they dutifully fulfilled their mission to provide a safe haven for many victims of domestic violence. They provided us a bunk bed and I got the top bunk. An old rocking chair was given to my mother, and my sister and I would sit on her lap while listening to the stories she would read from the shelter's collection of children's books. For the most part that was the extent to our furniture. We did not have many belongings because we could only pack what we could fit into the small police car that transported us, but Faith Mission readily and freely gave whatever clothes or supplies we needed. Most of the residents stayed in shared spaces and none of the kids were over the age of twelve. It was mostly a really young group with more kids than guardians.

There was a common bond between all the people staying at the shelter formed by ties of understanding, empathy, and a genuine concern for the others well-being. As for the staff, they were all my guardian angels. When we first moved into our new loft style refurbished basement, it was a relief, mostly because of the absence of my stepfather and also because there were plenty of kids my age there to play with. Being there transcended having a community; we had become family. Suddenly, I had gone from being in a dysfunctional and unstable home to a place where kids could make a few happy memories. A month and a half went by quickly, and as if to outdo themselves, the staff at Faith mission had planned something very special for me.

On the morning of my seventh birthday in the middle of September, I awoke excited. Life had slowed down, and I had forgotten my troubles. I was happy to be one year older. My mother's first words to me that day were 'Happy Birthday!' The weather was perfect, and somehow, I knew that it was going to be a special day. My morning was filled with lots of hugs and well wishes. The other children giggled under hushed breaths seeming to know something that I did not. Unbeknownst to me, my mother had partnered with the staff at Faith Mission to throw me a surprise party and I was definitely surprised. Who would have ever guessed that one could have such an experience and at such a place, but this was no ordinary homeless shelter. That day, when my mother led me to the playroom on the first floor, the children and their parents were waiting for me. They all lifted their hands and shouted, "Happy Birthday!"

My mother must have told them that my favorite cake was chocolate because they brought it out to me singing the 'Happy Birthday Song.' I felt like a normal kid, but it was not because of the cake or the birthday party. It was because I had a real family that loved me. After we all ate cake, they had one more surprise for me. From another room, they rolled out a brand new shiny red bicycle. My eyes must have opened to two times their original size. It was beautiful. I never had a bike before, and I did not even know how to ride it. They immediately began to teach me how to ride it there and in just about an hour, I was speeding, zipping, and flying circles around the playroom.

Looking back on my life I have accumulated many fond memories, but those of my childhood are some of the most special ones. With the help of Faith Mission, my mother, little sister, new baby brother, and I eventually received government housing after two months of staying at the shelter. When Rev. Howard Van Harlingen and Rev. Harold Barger first founded the mission in 1956, could they have known of all the lives that they would save or that what they built would still be saving lives to this very day? They had encountered numerous homeless individuals in their travels which led them from being remote spectators to being on the ground in the trenches. Their legacy and the bonds that I had formed with other homeless children have taught me that what homeless people are lacking more than nice clothes, warm meals, or even a home is someone who cares.

The National Center for Biotechnology Information reports that there are approximately ten million victims of domestic violence each year in America. Naturally, this affects the number of homeless youths each year who have to flee their homes. Fleeing, however, does not guarantee safety. There are countless risks associated with homelessness such as food insecurity, exposure to the elements, and the risk of being abducted or abused. Among the homeless, children are the most vulnerable to these kinds of dangerous situations. It is estimated that thousands of people die each year as a direct result of being homeless; the number of children deaths are unknown. If it had not been for the tender-loving virtuous people of Faith Mission, then I could have been one of them.

From my own experience, I have learned that there is a path to eradicating homelessness. Faith Mission is a 501 (c)(3) nonprofit. This means that they receive government funding and non-taxable income, but there are not enough shelters to currently meet the needs of the homeless. If we invest in our children, then we are investing in our future. Therefore, no child should ever have to worry about the impossible task of providing a safe place for themselves when there yet remains the option to fund worthy enterprises of philanthropy. Community outreach programs are the bulwarks of our citizens. We must not only stop there, but endeavor to make the shelter an interdiction to homelessness. Support for families is something everyone should readily have access to, and we need to educate the public to make them aware of how they can get access to such resources. If we can vaccinate over a hundred million citizens in less than half a year, if we can send a chimpanzee into space, then we should be able to provide safe environments to the very youths which will one day inherit this planet.

My seventh birthday and the gift of the red bicycle was more than a happy memory. It proved to me what humanity is capable of. Sometimes, in a shelter, all of your rooms are filled to capacity and there is no room for anyone else. By all appearances you have reached your limit, but that is when you dig deep and find that there is still a little room left…in your heart. That is when you can see what you did not see before. Suddenly, you realize there is a basement that no one is using. Humanity will never know what it is capable of unless we search our hearts and discover that there is room enough to care for a child. In this country there are two and a half million stories like mine that we have never heard; certainly, we can find a safe space for them.

While living with my stepfather, I was in constant fear every day for my sister, for my mother, for my unborn baby brother, and for myself. It was like falling into a dark pit with no bottom. No child should have to fear for the safety of their parent and no parent should have to fear for the safety of their child, but, too often, we sometimes do. I, however, am not the exception but the evidence that hope still exists. While at Faith Mission, I was experiencing childhood nirvana every day. The tears that brought us there were quickly replaced with the sounds of joy and laughter. It was like riding a bike for the first time.

"Where there is no vision, the people perish: but he that keepeth the law, happy is he." (Proverbs 29:18 KJV)

Tyra's Tears

Without understanding, who would survive? The cost of having understanding is high, but not as much as having none. This price for understanding is pain, which teaches us how it feels when the time comes for us to recognize someone else's pain. Most people just walk past when they see human suffering. Many cars drive past the homeless strangers living under bridges. It wasn't until I became homeless myself, that I really began to notice the many people around me who were suffering. It was because I knew how they felt.

There's a woman named Tyra who had been homeless for three years. For three years she said that she had not encountered one person who had been kind to her. Did Tyra become invisible? Was she in the middle of the dessert where no one could reach her? How could it be that there were no nice people for three years? Tyra knows; Tyra knows what it's like to be lonely. One doesn't have to be homeless to know what pain feels like, and it is because of that pain that one could empathize. There are so many people that need empathy; who need to be comforted by someone who knows how they feel. How could you comfort someone, if you didn't have the vision to see the pain? I couldn't count the cars that drove past Tyra; none of the people were able to see.

There is a time and place for everything, even pain. We need to hurt for the hurting. Curse or opportunity? There was once a time when a man walked this Earth who cared about the people. His conviction was so great that he died for it. Oh, if such people were not so rare. Who could find another Jesus? What would a world filled with likeminded people look like?

Prayer

Lord,

Make me like Jesus. If this is a prayer for pain, then let Your will be done. If I can learn from the pain, then let there be wisdom found in me; let not the pain be in vain. Help me to suffer in faith, then, I can see others and have understanding. Here I am calling on You Lord and praising You for Your love. Let love then, be my vision and let blind apathy be far from me. Jesus, take my pain and make me new.

Amen.

Looking for Beauty

It began when I said, "Yes."

"When are two people not equal?" God asked while leading me to the answer.

"When?" I asked.

"Sometimes, one person interprets a red image, or in other words, sees the color red. However, it is possible that out of a thousand people only one person sees the color purple in that same image. One might consider the difference in vision unique and beautiful, and another might consider the difference odd and against nature. Everyday people develop bias and prejudice, but art cannot be judged, for there is no standard to judge it by.

"Art by definition is an interpretation or in other words a vision of someone's mind. Everyone's mind works differently. No matter how hard two people try they will not agree on everything. At some point his red will inevitably encounter her refreshing shade of lavender."

"But when are two people not equal?" I asked again.

"When the doctors told you that you were Schizophrenic for seeing things in a refreshing shade of lavender."

After the conversation, I realized that I had been punishing myself for my uniqueness, when I should have been celebrating it. Our minds are works of art; therefore, be unique, be creative, and be yourself... even if they don't understand. Mental health is a real issue but being unique is a gift.

Prayer

Precious Lord,

The path we took is the one You chose, for You are before all things. You make the colors for us to see. Do we not interpret Your art? You see all colors; all points of view. We see in part, but You see the whole picture. Help us not to judge ourselves and realize that there are many perspectives around a table. Please help those who suffer from the stigmas of diagnoses. Help us to be kind to each other and kind to ourselves. Jesus, we need You.

Amen.

Delight in The Light

You Lord are my lighthouse. Your light will I follow when uncertainty and fear of the unknown attack me from all sides. My dearest is the only refuge I trust in during times of crisis. I will not toss aside God's gifts of faith, hope, and love for they are the treasures of my Father. The Great One gave me faith and taught me to have confidence in the love of God. I looked at hope, saw it with my own eyes, and yes, it was Jesus. Love was never hard to find, for God has been making all things work together in my favor since the day I was born. In all things there is God's love.

Why then, if the Lord is so near, do I always want more? Should it not be enough that my Savior is altogether one with my soul? Day after day I have to re-learn what it means to be in Your presence. To truly see Your face is to see many faces, for you are in the faces of Your children. Who could count Your children or the ways in which You express Yourself? I am honored and glad Lord that I have said thus, but who gave me the words? Was it not You? Lord, my blessings are like the raindrops.

I love You. These words cannot paint the picture in my heart, but it is like the window to a garden. I see You sitting there, and I want to join You. "Let's have a party and invite all of our friends," You say. I trust You. I believe the day is coming. Everyone is going to be there. What strange things You do making all my dreams come true. A little rain will follow with a ray of warmth from the sunlight. So too are my tears evaporated by Your sweet love. Love that's like honey.

Prayer

God,

I do not want the conversation to end, but to begin again. You lead and I'll follow. Whoever wants to join in the conversation should, and whoever wants to listen should. Both are gifts, especially when we realize that we are the instruments of Your voice. You can use anyone and anything to speak through. To be one with You is to have Your voice inside of us. May we all know and understand that Your voice is indeed inside of us.

Amen.

You Are My Wings

I have heard that God is love. Would a flower be beautiful if there was no love? Our love makes the flower beautiful. Otherwise, one would hardly notice a flower any more than they would a weed. But what if the weeds in our lives could be flowers? I believe they can be because I have known God to give me beauty for my ashes time and time again. One of the biggest blessings God ever gave me was pain, because from that pain, I grew wings. Now, I fly by God's love.

On occasion I prefer the cover over the content. I prefer roses and shun poison ivy. Both, however, are God's creation. Even more than that, both have God's love wrapped around them. The poison ivy teaches and the rose comforts. Both are necessary. Sometimes, pain is necessary. If you touch fire once it likely won't be that serious, but at least you'll learn to admire from afar. Pain becomes a necessary rite of passage for one who finds themselves in a kitchen. That first burn taught you to become aware of a lit stove.

Some people would watch the world burn, and every day will not be brightened up by a pretty flower. Flying is learning how to rise above adversity; to see the beauty in the weeds. Appreciating the low places in life takes you to the high places. The terrain won't always change, but your perspective can. Fly then, on wings of gratitude and you will never be held down. If we deeply consider it, then there was nothing that God made that is not beautiful, including you. Do not fear pain or adversity, because the only way you will soar highly above it, is by learning from the experience.

Prayer

Father,

Time and time again I have to surrender to Your guidance. How will I let go? Help me to believe that Jehovah Jireh is my provider. Teach me to see the beauty in the concrete, the compassion in the cracks, and the love in the rejection. I myself have been rejected, and yet I find that rejection is a part of life. We have choices; thus, we choose what to accept or deny. Thank You, for these wings of love.

Amen.

"God saw all that he had made, and it was very good. And there was evening, and there was morning—the sixth day." (Genesis 1:31 NIV)

Let it Go

David, a hungry man, sought refuge and help from the tabernacle of God on the day that Saul pursued him. He needed food, and the only bread that could be found was the bread set apart for the priests of God. This consecrated bread was to be used solely for the Lord's purpose, for the bread was on His alter. Uncommon uses for the sacred bread were altogether against the law and sinful. It was considered an act against God for anyone other than the priests to eat this bread. Yet, because God would prefer mercy over sacrifice, the bread was given to David by the priests; proving that love is not surrender to religious duties, but to the service of compassion and mercy.

I am the hungry man. As a gay man, my food is not the woman, for I cannot digest her. I did not crave her company, nor could I be satisfied by her. From childhood I went hungry hiding my desires, for I was told that they were an abomination. When finally, the man was brought before me, my hunger, like David's hunger, was satisfied. Does not God prefer mercy over sacrifice? Will he let the homosexual, who cannot control his or her desires, go hungry? No, for it is not good for one to be alone or to go hungry.

The LGBTQ community has been hungry for too long. We shame ourselves because of our appetites. No one shames the rest of God's creation for homosexual behavior; from insects to mammals there is a range of homosexual behaviors observed in the animal kingdom. The female Macaques, a species of primate, practices homosexuality almost exclusively in some areas. Would it not be considered animal cruelty if we stopped allowing animals like the female Macaques to mate with other females? Are not even the animals showing us that homosexuality is natural?

Prayer

Lord,

Your people hunger for romantic love. We look to You to be our God and feed us. Help us to not be ashamed. There are those of us that hate themselves and would rather go hungry. Help them; help them see that You prefer feeding us rather than letting us starve. Lord, we ask that You give us our desires and everything we need. Lord lastly, let us walk in the light of truth. Thank You Lord for these wonderful gifts.

Amen.

The Guilty

Of all the spirits I have encountered, Guilt, is the worst. If you can defeat Guilt, then you will overcome every evil. Guilt teaches you that you have to hide to protect yourself when the only danger is forgetting how to fly. It is better... to take the easy way up the mountain.

If you only forgive the deserving, then you are a poor judge, for God forgave without discrimination when He sacrificed His son for the forgiveness of our sins. Consider that before we ever had a chance to repent, Christ died. He forgave us before we ever earned our forgiveness. Could there be any guilt if we taught that we are born forgiven, or does God require payment? How then does a person earn forgiveness? God, knowing your mistakes from afar off, gave us Jesus on the cross not to condemn us, but to say, "I love you", to anyone who was listening.

If God loved us before we loved Him, then we were already forgiven. Guilt is not the absence of a mistake, but it is the presence of an accusation with the desire to condemn. Do not accuse the blood of Christ of not being enough to forgive everyone, for He died for everyone. Why then, does guilt remain? It is altogether confusion. Parents punish their children to teach them discipline, not to imply that they are worthless. God is not saying that you are worth less, but the cross says that you are worth more. When you realize your worth, no one can ever make you feel guilty again. It is time to forgive yourself because God already did. He never stops loving you no matter how many mistakes you make. Beware those who teach that forgiveness is given to the deserving, for no one earns love, yet God loves everyone... this is the heart of what Jesus taught.

Prayer

God,

Help us to accept Your love and learn to love ourselves. Free us from guilt and the desire to make others guilty. Thank You for the message of the cross. May we never forget.

Amen.

One Step at a Time

Everything begins with a step, but it is often that we lose track of the steps we took and even, that first initial step. Progress works this way. Robert H. Schuller once said, "You can know how many seeds are in an apple, but you can't know how many apples are in a seed." Planting a seed represents taking the first step and you don't always know, at first, where it will lead. If you want a tree, then you have to plant it. The tree won't come until it is in season. Maybe the solution to all of one's problems lies in what they can appreciate. If seeds can turn into trees, caterpillars into butterflies, and dreams into whole civilizations, then imagine what you and I could do with time.

We worry that we may not be enough; rich enough, smart enough, motivated enough, attractive enough, and anything else we use to measure worth. What makes the tree more important than the seed? The rocks on top of the mountain could not reach its peak without the rocks at the base. Do not despise small beginnings, feeling stuck, and not knowing what to do. The air taste's much sweeter on top of the mountain when you have to climb to get to there.

What if we stopped judging and measuring success? Things might slow down, but my guess is that they would speed up. Maybe we would stop comparing ourselves to everyone else. How would we know we were ever failing if we had no standard to compare ourselves to? It is not bad to have desires, but we should never feel less over what we don't have. If we do that, then we forget that life is a process. You see, what makes the air on top of the mountain taste so sweet are the steps.

Prayer

Great Spirit,

Thank You for Your many gifts. Over and over You show me something different, another possibility, and another way. Help us climb our mountains. Let us fly high above the treetops. Let us accomplish our dreams and more. Lord, I want to want what I have. Thank You for the time You have given me.

Amen.

Jesus once said, "Truly I tell you, if you have faith as small as a mustard seed, you can say to this mountain, 'Move from here to there,' and it will move. Nothing will be impossible for you." (Matthew 17:20 NIV)

Little

I think that one day humanity will wake up and say, "My goodness! A little light is all it took to create heaven on Earth." Yes, a little faith, a little hope, and a little love can create an Eden. Just as a candle gives light to a room, a connection with God enlightens and brings life. Wisdom is the enlightenment of God; it is ethical action that comes from the knowledge that good surpasses evil. A speck of light exists within the soul, and this light, which is of God, is our connection to heaven.

The path of the soul, which leads to life, understands that we are meant to try. We must try to have a relationship with God. We must try to be better than we were yesterday. And, we must try without knowing what it is we are trying to accomplish. Within the very essence of living, one finds that it is often that we live without knowing how to live, nevertheless, we try. This is the glory of humanity: that we reach towards the stars, to heaven.

Make no mistake, we will fail, and fail, and fail again. This will be a hard and an endless pursuit. The greatest of our gifts, our children, will not come into being without pushing against overwhelming obstacles. In the same way, what each one of us hopes to achieve will not happen unless we struggle for it. Once the children of the future are born, at great and greater costs, our blessings will be perfect and complete. A seed remains in the ground a long time before a tiny sprout becomes visible. We water the seed, the sun shines on it, and we provide good soil; yet, in all appearances nothing is happening. All the while, however, the seed is going through a great change. It grows, underneath the Earth, roots. If we use the seeds that God gave us, faith, hope, and love, we trust that what will grow must be good.

Prayer

A little faith, a little hope, and a little love
God is all I have. How is it that I never run out?
The future is bright. Teach me that a little speck
of light, however small it may be, can change the
world. Jesus, when He was born, was little. That
precious babe... taught us that great things can
come in small packages.

Amen.

Song of a Rain Dancer

It is easy to get discouraged waiting for the rain to come when there is only one cloud in the sky. Sometimes, the rain won't come until you first bring your umbrella. Believing in the dream can be harder that the dream itself, but it is the first step that begins a journey of a thousand miles. Beyond all our reasoning, God calls us to call things as they are. Remember, the angel called Gideon great when everyone else told him that he was small. Elijah predicted the rain without any of our present-day technology. Jesus said, "Destroy this temple, and I will raise it in three days."

Even so, what good is a sword if it is never used? The promises of God are a sword in our hands and yet, we hardly take the sword out its sheath by mentioning, declaring, and standing on God's promises. We believe what should be the source of everlasting joy; we believe that God is for us. Meditate on what you first believed. Jesus made a way for you and for everyone. You walk with the Lord even now as He guides you through the valley.

Shall we fear evil? No! For God is with us. Jesus shall never leave nor forsake you. Do not fear what tomorrow shall bring. You are healed. You are not addicted. You will get through this. What you have been waiting for to come need only be believed in. By faith ask and it shall be given unto you. He told you that if you should say to a mountain, "Be removed," that it will be.

I met a man named Victor who is no longer with us. The doctors said he had cancer, but he never accepted their diagnosis. When I meet Victor in good health one day after I have moved on, I hope to laugh with him and celebrate his victory. I want to be like this man. The Lord was his strength. Victor has risen.

Prayer

Dear Lord,

You call me by name. You know who I am. Therefore, let Your love guide my life. Bless You Lord.

Amen.

True Water

B eloved, one day you are going to see things differently. The way you look at yourself now does not realize oneness with the Creator. You dwell too much on what makes you different from everyone else. Then, not realizing it, you created imperfections when you rejected yourself. It is not your fault. There was always someone there to call you an abomination. Even when you try to like yourself, you cannot, because the voices will not go away; the voices of those who say that you are not good enough, ugly, and unlovable. One day, maybe today, your voice will rise above all the others and declare that you are God's creation. No mistakes were made.

Beloved, if you could just believe that, then you could have peace. Truly, the wars on the outside are just reflections of the wars on the inside. You will never be anyone other than yourself, so why not decide to love that person? The only other option is to wear a mask and pretend to be something you are not, which will be like drinking from the water of an oasis in the desert only to discover that it was a mirage.

Beloved drink, stand, and listen. Drink deeply from the waters of God's love for you. Stand in the canyon of God's unconditional acceptance towards you. Listen to God's voice above all others. God says, "You are fearfully and wonderfully made." If you hear God's voice, do not meet it with a deaf ear. There will never be a time when the voices of your critics sing truer and louder than the love song God played for you that day on Calvary.

Prayer

Dear God,

Thank You for making me divine. I am fiercely and fabulously made. Teach me how to love myself the way that You love me. Help the world see that being different is not an ugly thing, but something that is very beautiful. I trust You, Lord. I believe what You say. Still, I do not always like what I see when I look in the mirror. Sometimes, I am too afraid to look. Therefore, I acknowledge that I have a feeling of inadequacy. I bring to You my broken heart to heal and make stronger. I come before You humbly, as a student to a teacher. Show me what I have been missing all along.

Amen.

Shameless

"There is no such thing as shame."

Is what I will tell my daughter because there will come a day when evil tries to touch her. When God created the Garden of Eden, He made no shame. Everyone was naked or in other words they took no thought of covering themselves. Adam and Eve created shame when they consented to the thought that something was wrong with them or to be more precise, they saw evil in themselves. Evil has a face and it is shame, but unless we agree to it, there is no such thing as shame.

Shame gave birth to fear, for when Adam and Eve saw themselves, they ran to fix what was natural. Fear gave birth to pain, for they could not bear it and covered themselves. Then comes discontent followed by bitterness. Envy, greed, and gluttony are all the names of things that followed after shame; but if there is no shame where are her children? Without shame can there be condemnation?

Let the Lord judge. "There is therefore now no condemnation for those who are in Christ who walk not according to the flesh, but according to the Spirit." (Romans 8:1) We are not just flesh but have the will and emotions of God living in us and through us. Therefore, where God is no shame can be found. One either agrees to shame or chooses to believe that it does not exist. God loves everyone, so do not shame the one God loves. To be in Christ is to be in His love and Jesus loves you, is in you, and One. How can anyone make you feel anything without your permission?

Prayer

Lord God,

Hear me. I want to love myself as You love me. I do not want to measure my worth and by so doing teach others to do the same. Free everyone from this insanity. Who should feel ashamed if the only reason it existed was because one walked away from their divine self? To You Lord is where I will go when voices rise condemning me, for You alone can judge me. Praise You for Your glorious love, for You will not put me to shame.

Amen.

"Refrain from anger and turn from wrath; do not fret—it leads only to evil." (Psalm 37:8 NIV)

Face to Face with Evil

This is the story of a young boy's dream. He came face to face with what some would call darkness, others The Beast, and few who see themselves. Some things, however, you cannot judge by appearances. In this dream the boy was flying over a forest when he suddenly came across a certain figure amongst the trees. At first glance the boy saw what looked like a black werewolf. Upon closer inspection the boy saw bloodlust in the creature's eyes. Standing on its hind legs with teeth bared and reaching towards the boy as though it could touch him, the eyes of this black wolf held pure darkness. The boy had no fear when he looked in the creature's eyes, even though it was looking for his death. Instead, the boy reacted in disgust. It was as if he was smelling decaying flesh for the first time, but unbearably worse.

The boy rejected the creature and said aloud, "Jesus devour it." A couple of moments passed, and the beast completely disappeared from vision. A couple more moments passed, and The Beast reappeared as a crying infant. This dream was only one part of a much deeper conversation. What the boy saw was the mask of suffering. A crying baby was all Jesus left. He devoured the hatred and left the baby. Why? Perhaps the answer is different for each of us. There is, however, a clue. The boy said, "Devour it."

Indeed, there was nothing left of the werewolf; Jesus devoured it. This means that the crying baby was something different. The darkness was only the mask; thus, it was destroyed. The baby was left behind because it was not darkness; rather, its suffering had created the wolf. God is showing us that hurt people... hurt people. If a man wears a mask and becomes someone else, he is an actor. We are all acting, but not everyone is acting like themselves.

Prayer

Lord,

I want to see what You see. Give me vision and the strength to carry the vision. Teach me how to come in and go out or how to walk wisely. Devour my mask and the mask of my neighbor. Heal the suffering and bring peace, joy, love, and laughter. Praise You Lord, the one who reveals secrets. Truth and insight are Your gifts. When I seek you, I find You.

Amen.

A Flicker of Hope

Hope is what the world needs. We are losing so much, so fast. For some, it is their darkest days. Paradoxically, it is when things are at their darkest, when vision shows you a picture of something horrible, that somehow, the tinniest speck of light offers hope. There is one treasure in my mind that I esteem more than anything. It is a memory of about three years ago and begins in a time much like this, in chaos. Three years ago, in the summer of 2017, I was walking aimlessly down an unknown street in the middle of the night. I was looking for Jesus, but I had no idea of where to start. With only the moon and stars to guide me, I walked for hours in unrecognizable neighborhoods. Some people might have considered me heartbroken, but it was more than that; I was used to being broken. This was a boy looking for the light in a pitch-black maze. My faith was fighting harder than it ever had in looking for someone I knew very little about.

"Go home," it was a whisper. I submitted to the voice and remember feeling a strange peace the whole way home. I should have been lost, but I made it home exerting no more effort than it took to walk. After my long walk, I went to sleep and had a dream that I have thought about every day since that night. Jesus was waiting for me in a beautiful garden sitting on a rock. There were flowers every one or two feet apart from each other in various colors ranging from lavender to tangerine. I walked through these flowers to the loveliest tender loving person wearing a robe of pure white.

As I got close to Him, I could actually feel His love, not just for me, but for everyone. That, in and of itself, was the greatest gift I ever remember receiving. In that love, was the hope that I had with all my heart been searching for. This love did not care about your religion, face, or shame. This love was the reason, my reason, and my hope. When I looked at His face I plainly did not understand. In a single moment, His face had the appearance of everyone and anyone you could ever imagine wearing a modest half-smile. If you want to see hope, then look in the mirror and smile, because to me, Jesus looks like you.

Prayer

Oh Creator God,

Holiest of Holies, Your majesty cannot be put into words. Guide these hearts that gather close to You today. Let us find hope when all seems lost. Let us remember that our precious hope is inside all of Your children who were made in Your likeness. Let us remember that our hope is Your love.

Amen.

Ripples in a Small Pond

Consider peace. Lao Tzu gave the formula for peace when he said, "If there is to be peace in the world, there must be peace in the nations. If there is to be peace in the nations, there must be peace in the cities. If there is to be peace in the cities, there must be peace between neighbors. If there is to be peace between neighbors, there must be peace in the home. If there is to be peace in the home, there must be peace in the heart." The individual directly affects the world. When there is war in the heart, there is war in the world. Each individual has the power to affect this world positively or negatively, and either way, we have to live with the consequences.

When a person has no values, the world will have less values, and in the end, our world will have less value. We are plagued with corrupt world leaders because it is us who are creating them. Unless we realize that we are all living in a world made smaller by our connectedness and that one pebble causes ripples in the whole of a small pond, then the world will never be at peace and the surface of the water will never be still. When you do not value life, all life, everything alive will be in danger from you.

The gravity cannot be underestimated because your life and what you choose to do with it, matters. Believe that you can affect this world, change this world, and better this world. We are contagious creatures. Our love is just as contagious as our hate. The common denominator behind Lao Tzu's formula was you and me.

Prayer

Divine Spirit,

As the world suffers from one plague after another, we realize that we are all connected. Help us to live with love towards all that You made. Give us the grace to love ourselves and be at peace. Bless You Great Spirit.

Amen.

The Weapon of Love

Many of us are hurting, and the cries for justice are being heard from every corner, from every home, and around the world. In our pursuit of justice, the words of Martin Luther King ring in a pitch so clear, and so pure that they must be remembered. In honor of his memory, and in all of the lives that we have lost to senseless violence, I want to offer a small quote from Martin Luther King.

He says, "As you press on for justice, be sure to move with dignity and discipline using only the weapon of love. Let no man pull you so low as to hate him. Always avoid violence. If you succumb to the temptation of using violence in your struggle, unborn generations will be the recipients of a long and desolate night of bitterness. And your chief legacy, to the future, will be an endless reign of meaningless chaos." Let's do our best. Let's stand together with dignity and discipline to preserve the legacy of the great Martin Luther King and this great nation.

Prayer

Great Spirit,

We are a world turning in our beds, never finding comfort. Our pain comes from wounds too deep to reach. For countless nights we have cried ourselves to sleep, but never finding rest. How long will the wicked be allowed to oppress us? How long will we look for justice, and find only disappointment in her place? There is nothing new under the sun. Therefore, we will praise You. Our God is a God of justice, equity, and righteousness. By Your word You created the Earth and all that dwell therein. You established the oceans and told them how far they could go. Wisdom is in Your right hand and understanding is in Your left.

Let every voice praise the Lord! We do not call on one who does not hear, does not see, or does not feel. You are righteous, and Your love endures forever. Praise You God, for Your blessing is for the righteous, and Your curse is for the wicked. May we honor You by never doubting You. May we be faithful to You as You have been faithful to us.

Amen.

"And the Lord said, 'Do you do well to be angry?'" (Jonah 4:4 ESV)

That Which is Easier

The cost of unforgiveness is anger. The cost of anger is bitterness. The cost of bitterness is hatred. The cost of hatred is division. The cost of division is war. And the cost of war is death. If you do not want to forgive, then ask yourself, "Do I prefer anger, bitterness, hatred, division, war, and death?" Nelson Mandela gave the metaphor, "Resentment is like drinking poison and then hoping it will kill your enemies." In the end, your emotions can do the greatest damage and you become your own enemy. It is better then, to forgive…and live!

There is a certain Buddhist parable about two monks who took a vow never to touch women. The elder monk breaks his vow and carries a woman in need across a river. He forgave himself for breaking the vow when he decided to touch her and was able to help someone else because of it. The younger monk saw this and was upset at the elder monk for breaking his vow. When the younger monk questioned his elder about his actions, the elder monk replied, "I set her down hours ago by the side of the river. Why are you still carrying her?" Emotions can be very heavy, and it is difficult to carry a burden for too long. Forgiving is hard, but not as hard as carrying a load for your entire journey.

Forgive others and forgive yourself because the alternative is even more painful than the offense that caused the pain in the beginning. To love is to forgive. It is not easy to love an enemy, but only love can change an enemy into a friend. Only love has the power to heal a broken heart. We love, not because it is convenient, but because everyone's survival depends on it. Therefore forgive, love, and live.

Prayer

Spirit of Love,

Liberate our hearts. Guide our thoughts. Forgiveness is hard when there is no desire for it, but we all crave a better world. We often ask for Your love not seeing that there was a reason why You gave us hearts. If we are to be Your hands and feet, then show us how to be Your heart as well. At some point, we all ask for forgiveness. Help us to give freely what has been freely given to us. Bless You Great One, for Your love is life itself.

Amen.

Never Alone

God is a companion more desirable than a million friends. It is better to be alone with God than it is to be surrounded with much company and no fellowship with Him. He is the friend that never leaves you and never forsakes you. Who is a better friend than God? I have had many friends, and many times we parted ways because of our differences, but God will never abandon you. Why should I be lonely when I am not alone? God is everywhere. Where I am God is. He is with me on top of the mountain, and He is with me when I am in the lowest valley. In the shadow of death God is with me; therefore, I will not fear.

No one can make you feel lonely without your consent. If you are convinced that you are alone it is because you agreed to the suggestion. Seek God and you will find Him. A person with a million friends has little remembrance of their need of God. I would rather be popular with God than be popular with mankind. This is not to say that companionship is not to be desired. Companionship is good. When we do good unto others it is as though we are doing it unto the Lord. Fellowship is not to be forsaken, and the opportunity is a precious gift from above. However, to have fellowship with God is far more desirable of an opportunity.

To have a lot of company is a gift, but so too is isolation. Many friends bring much happiness. Isolation gives you the opportunity to sit down with the King. Pray for understanding. Isolation is not a curse, but an opportunity. The love of God far surpasses romance. Intimacy with God develops when one is alone with Him. His love is the greatest love; therefore, prefer God.

Prayer

My God and dearest friend,

Show us that You are here right next to us. Comfort us with Your words of love. Teach us wisdom and incline our hearts towards Your presence daily. Thank You for never leaving us. When I am aware of Your presence, all is well with my soul. Keep our eyes on You always. Bless You Lord for these gifts of time with You and companionship. We love You God.

Amen.

The Greatest Joy

Nothing compares to the gift of love. I hope for love, I dream of love, and I meditate on love. Love has shaped my thoughts and desires since the day I first formed my earliest memories. My mother would hug me, so tight, and it was as if the love from her very soul was being poured into me. Love was my first impression and my first gift. Naturally, I developed a taste for it. I discovered that the only thing comparable to receiving love was giving love. In this way, love becomes a dance with many partners moving to the rhythm of the heart.

Sometimes, when we feel alone, we forget how to dance. We forget that dancing requires taking a step the same way love does. My mother showed me the beauty of love and I have never seen her wanting love. She always got back what she gave in the same way she gave what she got from her mother. The first step is always the most difficult in the way that new things can be scary. Once you have the courage to dance, however, your body takes over and you groove to sounds no one else can hear. "Live with love," that is what my heart tells me. Give when you are able, forgive while you can, be grateful, and always, move forward.

No matter how much love hurts because it is delayed or denied, to love and be loved will leave you celebrating in awe and amazement. God gave us hearts so that we would discover the road to happiness lies in what we feel. Without love there can be no beauty, joy, or inner peace, for these things are distinctions of the heart, not the mind. To breath is to live, but to love is to be alive. My mother wanted the best for me and said, "I love you," every time she protected me, helped me, and wiped away my tears. I am my mother's son and I have the same power as she, and I give it to you freely. This power is the knowledge of how to simply take the first step of a beautiful dance. The first step... is giving the love you want to see in the world to others.

Prayer

Holy Mother,

Show us the greatest love. Take our hand and lead us onto the dance floor. Turn our walking into dancing. Bless You.

Amen.

"If you give to others, you will be given a full amount in return. It will be packed down, shaken together, and spilling over into your lap. The way you treat others is the way you will be treated." (Luke 6:38 CEV)

Going the Distance

Right now, is a very important time in my life because I am learning what it means to persevere. It's almost half-way through September of 2020 and I find myself spending time with my Grandmother Lena who is passing from this life on to the next. Today, I was singing to her Amazing Grace, and as I was singing, I was looking at her face. Most would see a very tired woman, but I saw something more. What I saw, was a woman who has conquered this life, surround by her children, and a legacy of what it means to be someone who tries and sacrifices. More importantly, I recognized the treasures that she has given us.

My grandmother's love created a family with unbreakable bonds. She has given each of us an appreciation for each other. Grandmother Lena is a mother, matriarch, teacher, friend, and more. If she would have given up early in life, then none of us would be here today. By living her life, she gave us ours. As her grandson, I am filled with gratitude because she has showed me something that I can admire. Namely, the reason to why we try so hard in this life to live. I've learned, through her, that we do not live this life only for ourselves, but for each other as well.

I am less than half her age and already there have been many times in life when I wanted to quit, give up, and stop living. At the time, I did not realize that I would not only be cutting my life short, but so too the life of everyone I never got to give the gift of my life. Our lives are gifts, especially when we can share them with others. There is so much life has to offer. My grandmother has given us so much. In honor of her I can give this fundamental lesson: if life makes you tired, then you are doing something very, very right.

Prayer

Giver of life,

Bless You for our lives, for the many gifts that life brings, and for what we get to leave behind. Thank You for my grandmother's life and for the lessons she has given me. Help me to pass them on to others who are thinking about giving up. May she remind us that life can make you tired, and that that is ok. Thank You Lord, for Your boundless love.

Amen.

The Beautiful Race

Pain is the proof of progress. One who runs a race, and is tired at the end, earns their medal and their celebration. Life is a race, not against an opponent, but against yourself. In the end, you either leave disappointed or celebrating. The medal you earn is the gratitude you gain from everything the race taught you. All forms of pain: loss, grief, and anguish make getting to the finish line so worthwhile. I want to be tired, but I know that I am not tired yet because there is so much more that I can do. We all run our race, but how we run is what makes the race special.

I could give up. I could quit. But if I did, then could I say that I was truly alive? Without running, and instead by giving only half of my heart, I would have only half a reward. Every lap of my years lived on this Earth, measured not by quantity but quality, changes me. At first, I was scared of change, but growth is a change that I now desire. There are growing pains with the absence of regret, because the more I grow into a new creature, the better I am able to run my race.

There is no wisdom without pain nor gratitude without some struggle for it. Things that come easy are easily forgotten, but things that are hard to come by are hardly discarded. See then, that greater joy awaits the one with the greater struggle. It is difficult to live a life that I can be proud of, and for that, I am grateful. Our elders deserve honor, because they are the ones who have been where we are trying to go. There are many races, but only one you, so run your race your way and wave to me from the finish line.

Prayer

Bless You Father,

For You breathed life into me and showed me what I can do with the air. You taught me how to cherish each breath and taught me not to waste it. I want to be tired, but only when it is time to be because I am really enjoying this race. It is a satisfying struggle in which I will one day find myself celebrating. "Hallelujah," is what I will say when I meet You at the finish line!

Amen.

Healing a Heart

If you want to shine a light in the darkest places of a person's heart, then do so with empathy. Be poor with the poor, sick with the sick, and hurt with the hurting as one who thoughtfully considers their struggle. Even a stranger can comfort another; how much more is it to be comforted by a friend who recognizes your pain. It is easier for two people to communicate when they speak the same language. When one is able to speak with empathy, she is able to meet those suffering where they are and connect with them through her understanding. Reaching the heart is a matter of closing the distance between our thoughts and emotions.

With our minds we can recognize when another person is hurting, but it is with our hearts that we truly understand. A journey is more easily traveled with a guide. Comparatively, it is harder to lead someone somewhere you have never been to. A doctor studies the condition of the body before he treats it. Likewise, we as helpers are better equipped when we understand who we are trying to help. Empathy is not always possible, but the act of making the attempt to understand another's pain is true friendship. Sometimes, being a friend means that it is better to listen when we do not know what to say.

When we do not understand how a person is feeling, we can admit it without fear. Just the desire of wanting to help is a great gift. For some, the only thing they ever lacked was having a friend who cared. Feelings are powerful; they are the passion behind our prayers and actions. Your good will can save a life, change a life, and create a better life for another. Don't be overwhelmed by what you can't do; instead, bring your concerns to God, for nothing is too hard for the One who is all powerful and all knowing. Love is the greatest expression of empathy, for realizing when another person needs it…is true understanding.

Prayer

Spirit of love,

Grant us insight. This may mean that we have to struggle to understand the struggle of others, however, we are grateful for wisdom. Show us the way to healing so that we may be able to show others. Let love shine in the dark places and create in us peaceful and joyous spirits. Bless You Great One.

Amen.

"'Come on!' Jesus said. Peter then got out of the boat and started walking on the water toward him. But when Peter saw how strong the wind was, he was afraid and started sinking. 'Save me, Lord!' he shouted." (Matthew 14:29-30 CEV)

In God's Hands

In my darkest days, I did not keep my eyes focused on God. I lost sight of what is important. Fear was at my left and worry was at my right. God was before me, but I did not hope. I lost the faith. Howbeit that Jesus was there to save me from drowning. Peter was sinking, not only in the water, but in his own doubt as well. Though he took his eyes off Jesus, the Lord rescued him.

I am not defeated nor am I ashamed. Instead of giving room to vanity I will remember what it was like to point the gun at myself. I was in a desperate situation and seemingly hopeless. When I pulled the trigger that should have been the end of my life. Something did die that day though it was not me. It was the thought that I was in control. If there was one thing God kept me alive for it was to say that. We are not in control.

Praise God, because the One who is in control happens to be madly in love with us.

Many times, we will encounter storms of various kinds: unwelcomed change, illness, and even death. There are too many things that could go wrong to never think about it. Instead of seeing your situation, for just a moment, picture Jesus as you see Him in your heart. Now look at Him. Keep looking at Him. He's not going to let you drown. I will tell you again, Jesus is not going to let you drown. You may lose your life, but you will never lose your soul so long as God is keeping it.

Prayer

Abba Father,

We cry out, "deliver us." These winds of change have blown me over. The waves threaten to drag me to the depths of despair. I have tried everything on my own and all I got for it was heartache. Reach into my soul Lord. Pull me out of the waters. Put me on solid ground. Give me the will to live. It is all I can do to even pray. If it were anything other than You, I would dare not hope anymore for fear of losing one more thing.

My Love keep our eyes on You. If we should look to our left, be at our left. If we should look to our right, be at our right. Be ever before us on all sides and may we see You. Bless You Lord, for You will not suffer my soul to dwell in hell. As long as I have breath, I will believe that in the town of Bethlehem a child was born. His name was Jesus.

Amen.

The Power of Prayer

Prayer is not the reciting of a magic spell; it is a conversation with God. Words do not have any power in and of themselves, but when we with sincerity come humbly to God, He draws near to us because He loves us. Eloquence does not make a prayer more powerful, but God who is powerful makes us, who are weak apart from Him, blessed according to our righteousness. If our requests are good, then our Father in heaven will bestow upon us His power and authority. Nothing will be impossible for us because God can do all things.

One does not make demands of a king if he values his life. Consider then, that a king is higher than his servant. Just as a king's position is the highest in the land, our King who is Christ, has thoughts much higher than ours. God does not need our understanding to answer a prayer; it is us who need His understanding to be the answer to our prayers. You may have a plan or a solution, but God knows the right way to solve a problem. With humility, consider asking God to "help" without feeling you have to tell God how He should help, for His ways our not our ways and His thoughts are not our thoughts. (Isaiah 55:8) Remember that He is King over all of creation, who knows what we are going to ask before we speak and has prepared aforehand the best answer to our prayers.

We do not have to come up with long prayers nor do we have to figure out what to pray for. God already knows what we need, and often what we want differs from what we need. You may know what you need, but God knows how and when to give it.

We should ask for the impossible, for God is willing and able to do it, and have the humility to submit to the will of God if things do not go the way we expect them to. Sometimes we have made prayer harder than it has to be.

Prayer

Dear Lord, you are the God over all. We pray that you protect every child from the harm that surrounds them. Please provide a safe community and a safe haven for them to turn to in times of trouble, so that they may live long days filled with Your love and joy.

Amen

The Right Road

All those who commit themselves to the ways of love, being long suffering, will enjoy the rewards. Keep your eyes on the prize, like a mother who for the sake of her unborn child endures labor pains. Once the offspring of your commitment to love is received, great suffering is replaced by far greater joy. Farmers commit their lives to their crops, enduring hardships with much patience, because they hope to gain a harvest. When all you can see is dirt covering your hopes, it is easy to lose confidence. However, the dirt is the opportunity for the growth of the seed. The farmer knows that the seed is planted, and the mother knows that her child won't come without great effort. Love is the right road to travel on and leads us to the sweetest place.

As one travels, one will know that they are on the right road by the appearance of opposition. Before the destination is reached, do not be alarmed by the appearance of a black werewolf and expect to be bitten. The attack will not be by a literal werewolf, but rather, what it represents. It means that you have almost reached your destination. Be ready, for a journey is not completed without facing one's demons. Travel in confidence, because if love is the compass directing you, then God will be the One fighting on your behalf.

The end of a journey is the start of a new journey. Every beast that was fought was training for the new journey. Acquiring an education is an endless journey, for there will always be something to learn. From year to year, one travels through many seasons. There is a season for being a student and a season for being a teacher; a time to prepare and a time to travel. Always let love be your north star. Examine yourself, not to second guess, but to affirm that you have not followed the wrong star. Heaven is on the other side of long suffering, but there is no suffering there, only long gladness.

Prayer

Abba God,

Help us. Make a way for love. If ever we find ourselves hating the wrong things or loving the wrong things, shine brightly before us like a star so that we may return to the right road. In Jesus name we pray,

Amen.

"Even though I walk through the valley of the shadow of death, I will fear no evil, for you are with me; your rod and your staff, they comfort me." (Psalm 23:4 ESV)

Through the Valley

Sometimes, it is all too easy to see the work of the enemy. It feels like being caught in the rain without an umbrella even though you packed one. Sometimes Lord, I just want to give up. I feel the urge to quit creeping up on me with each temptation Satan brings. As soon as I say, "I've had enough," it is like the ground beneath me starts to tremor and all hopes of peace and balance are lost.

The Sprit answers, "Here I am, I never left. I had to bring you back to me. Without realizing it you got tied up in the cares of the world. If I let you have your way, then you'd be paying a far greater price. It is out of love that I allowed you to suffer."

Tony Evans once said, "Sometimes, God lets you hit rock bottom so that you will discover that He is the rock at the bottom." Trials bring us closer to God because a weary heart makes a greater demand on God. I know that the good I do is not in vain; therefore, though I weep, I will love Him. Even if my body breaks, my heart will sing a song of thanksgiving. And if tears shall flow like streams, I shall lift up my voice and cry out to you for help. No devil, thorn in the flesh, or root of bitterness will deceive me for I know who my God is.

He is my strength and my defense. She is my Mother. He is my Brother. My Lord comforts me when my wounds have become far too many to number. My God is love, and although there is too much love for me ever to be able to comprehend, I will spend eternity learning Her ways.

Prayer

Dear Lord,

I have tried not giving up. I have tried not getting angry or bitter. Yet I fail time after time. Allow me to be faithful at the bottom so that when I meet You, I will have no regrets. Let us remember that not everything is the devil; sometimes, it's just life. Jesus in Your precious name I pray,

Amen.

Don't Quit

Can you hear the voice of God telling you to listen? She is beckoning you. Come, gather and listen. Hasn't it been a long journey? For everyone it has. Breathe in and exhale. You can't die now. Don't give up and don't faint. God knows that you suffer, and it's because you chose love. Whether romantic, forbidden, or brief love has a cost. At some point we either bury the ones we love or are buried by the ones we love. God grieves for Her child whose voice is unheard because no one stops to listen.

"I am hurting," you say.

The Spirit whispers, "Don't die, I won't let you die. Because you have been fighting… fighting for this long. You have a dream, and the only one who can stop it is you. For I am for you. I have chosen you. You are my child. I will give you strength. I will give you the courage to not give up on your dream. Remember that courage is not the absence of fear, but the heart that has the faith to take a step anyways. If you can take a step, then you have more strength then you know."

The hardest part was the longing: wanting to receive the love that I was giving to everyone else. I too have mourned a loved one. All this is vanity because love is worth fighting for, even dying for. Consider the lengths to which Christ went, all for the sake of love. Do we count Him as having erred? Of course not. We endure as Christ did, for the sake of love. Don't give up. The day in which the Lord comes for Her children is fast approaching.

Prayer

Prince of Peace,

Give us Your strength. Take the burdens we aren't meant to bear. Come for Your children who long to be with You where You are. Let us find You here and bring heaven to us. Bless our eyes to see the Christ Child in each of us and bring healing to the world. Thank You Lord,

Amen.

Strength

What is strength? Do you think you are not strong because you cry, fall down, or at times so vulnerable it feels as though you could break at any moment? Well you're wrong. Jesus cried in front of everyone because the people He cared about were suffering, but was He weak? No.

Jesus fell to His knees in the Garden of Gethsemane because He knew that He was about to die. Was He weak even then? No, He most certainly was not. Was Jesus ever more vulnerable than when He was on the cross?

He was vulnerable, but He was not weak!

Just because we are human, like Jesus was human, does not negate the fact that "greater is He who is in us, then he who is in the world." (1 John 4:4) Strength is not the absence of weakness, or our humanity; it is the presence of a holy and righteous God who lives inside of us.

Prayer

Our Holy Father,

Grant us Your strength. We need You now more than we ever have. Teach us that Your strength is made perfect in our weakness. We are fragile yes, but only in body. Our souls contain that speck of light that shines in the darkness. You told us to overcome darkness with light. Shine on us, shine from within, and cast out every shadow.

Bless You Lord, for we shall live forever. Your faithfulness to us is eternal, even though comprehending such love is forever out of our reach.

Thank You Lord, for Your many gifts including weakness. For weakness isn't weak when You are near. Quite the opposite; our weaknesses shows us that we can't rely on ourselves alone, but on You. We love You Father. Let Your will be done. In Jesus name we pray,

Amen.

Faith Over Fear

The closer one gets to God, the further away one gets from a spirit of fear. Consider, Sir Isaac Newton. He postulated the Laws of Motion. In the first law, he observed that an object in motion tends to stay in motion, and conversely, an object at rest tends to stay at rest. Unless the object is acted upon by a force it tends to remain in motion or at rest. The law applies to the mind inasmuch as it does an object, for peace and anxiety are states of rest and motion that can be affected by a force. If the human will can be considered a force, then we can affect our own minds either positively or negatively. The prophet Isaiah observed this law well before Newton when he said, "You will keep him in perfect peace, whose mind is stayed on You, because he trusts in You."

Imagine your favorite spot; it could be a church, in the arms of a loved one, or your favorite scenery. The whole time you are there you are relaxed, but then, you leave and your focus changes. As you head home, your mind starts to drift towards your responsibilities, body aches, and appearance. Suddenly, you become stressed to the point of anxiety. Your mind goes from rest to motion. When you were focused on God, your loved one, or the beauty of your surroundings you were fine. It was not until outside forces began to distract you that your mind began to race, and you became fearful.

Our battle with fear today is the same as Peter's battle thousands of years ago. As long as Peter kept his eyes on Jesus, he was able to walk on water. It was not until he stopped looking at Jesus, and instead focused on the winds and waves, that he started to sink. The love of God is a force, and the more we seek His love, the greater our rest will be. Exercise your faith by seeking God in every circumstance and on every occasion, for His love will free you from worry. In times of uncertainty be certain that you can trust God to make all things work together for your good. (Romans 8:28)

Prayer

Holy Father,

We trust that You are good, and we know that there is nothing to fear. If ever our minds should wander, we trust that like a good shepherd, You will bring us back. Teach us to exercise our faith by pursuing You constantly. Bless You Lord for putting our minds at rest. In Jesus we trust,

Amen.

"Do not forget to show hospitality to strangers, for by so doing some people have shown hospitality to angels without knowing it." (Hebrews 13:2 NIV)

Everyday Angels

Everyone has a guardian angel. No one is left alone, even for a moment. Angels are often in disguise, usually invisible, but I have learned that angels have many forms. A close friend, parent, or even a teacher can be an angel that God sent to help you along your way. I have known a couple of very loyal cats that I consider to be angels. Also, I have come across great teachers who have guided me as only an angel would. The word angel comes from the Greek word angelos, which usually refers to a messenger of God. What every angel has in common is that they help one better understand the message of God, which in one word is: love.

I strive to be an angel wherever I go, to carry the solitary message of love. The message does not always have to be said. Sometimes, it is more important to be the message. This means that my actions speak louder than my words. More often than not, it is the small day to day actions that go unnoticed but speak the loudest. Small deeds like giving someone a hug, a smile, or even something as small as holding the door open for a stranger offer me the most opportunities to share the message. Small deeds cannot be underestimated because each time I show love, I share God's message.

We have always considered angels to be glowing beings with wings, but it is just as important to consider our everyday angels too. They are our health care workers, our soldiers, and our working-class citizens. Without these people our society would collapse. Consider that God's love for us is so great that he gave us so many angels to defend us, guide us, and encourage us. It is not wrong to think so highly of such people, but it is neglectful not to. For they watch over you as they watch over me. Today, we pray for angels without noticing that the prayer was already answered before we even asked.

Prayer

Father God,

Thank You for giving us so many people who are sharing Your message of love daily. Teach us to acknowledge them and appreciate them as they should be. Bless You Lord, for the angels in whom You delight have surrounded us. May we shine and be a blessing as they do.

Amen.

God Loves Everyone

For years, I struggled with Religious Stockholm Syndrome. Normally, Stockholm Syndrome is defined as having feelings of affection or trust towards one's captor. It is possible, however, to be held hostage by one's religion insomuch that I was trapped in a cage of fear by the teaching that I was going to go to hell because I was gay. My captor, as it turns out, never even existed. Instead of getting to know God myself, I trusted mankind's image of God, and it was this image that held me prisoner. The image promised me love as long as I obeyed without question. I was a child when I developed a Religious Stockholm Syndrome that was generational, and I was taught to confuse prejudice with love from people who were suffering from the same things I was.

How often does mankind confuse prejudice with love because we believe it is what God wants? Would the Creator of the universe think as a man who lives but for a short time? Or what does it mean to show love to another? No one can live our lives for us; therefore, we need to ask our own questions and seek out the answers. I would never believe someone who said, "I love you," if they were trying to destroy me. Ironically, I use to accept that God discriminated, and I called it good. Even worse than what I was doing to myself, was passing my degradation and Religious Stockholm Syndrome to others.

It is long overdue that humanity examined the impossibility of a God of love having a human disposition of prejudice. You do not have to pray like I pray or think like I think to get my love. I should hope to believe that God is better than I, and would in nowise, love you less than me. Anger comes from unresolved pain, and it is sad, that many have allowed their anger to become hate. But their story does not have to be your story. You can face the pain and give it the one thing it needs, and that is love.

Prayer

Abba God,

Save us from the pain, from the helplessness, from the loneliness, from the rejection, and from the anger that turns into hatred. Break every cycle of discrimination in the world. Teach us who You really are, for we long to know You. Free us from all bondage. Bless You Lord. In You we trust.

Amen.

Priceless Dirt

God makes everything work together. They are held together by love. We have heard that God is love, and if all things are affected by this love, they are connected by the same love. All things work together because God's love reaches every place. If God is in every place, then is anything common? Are our lives or the lives of those growing from the ground, swimming in the sea, or crawling in the sand common?

When one stop's and listens to the voice of harmony between bird and sky, they hear the song of The Musician that causes life to dance. God doesn't need to come down; this Being is already here. To see God is knowing how to look. Everything is precious. What is a soul and why do so few have one? Equality is often found at a steep price, but prejudice is easily purchased. Love is free and for everyone or it isn't love at all.

In essence, God's will lives through everything. From a grain of sand to the majestic elephant, both are sustained and carried by God's love; what He created He loved. The Lord has many faces depending on how one looks. To see God in a grain of sand is to see the universe, for He created them both. If God makes all things work together, then it is because we are connected by the same thread. Love made the world; nothing was made without love.

Prayer

Beautiful Lord,

How does one love everything? A garden must be kept by its master, so let everything flourish like Eden. The world does not see You even though You are all around. Open our hearts so that we can truly see. If we measure the worth of something, dry up the thought at its source. Let this conversation over which is less and which is more fade from memory. I'm grateful for Your waters which connect us all. Nothing can live unless they are nourished by these waters. The Spirit is everywhere and so too is heaven, for where God is no falsehood exists. Darkness is as light to You.

Amen.

Don't Define Me

Today, it is ironic that from nothing comes everything. Nothing is not the absence of something, rather, it is no thing. To prove this, consider the following question: what is the face of a man? We have all decided that the face of a man is his appearance from the top of his forehead to the bottom of his chin. Our civilization has made a universal definition for something that is anything but universal. For everyone has a face, but everyone does not have the same face. Thus, there are different faces, but one definition for it. Therefore, the definition of a face is no one thing, or appearance, but encompasses everything we know about faces. It is nothing, but everything.

There are many different shades of black, however, I am not characterized by my complexion; I am merely referred to as black. The sky has a plethora of appearances, but regardless of whether it is day or night, the air above is referred to as the sky. Rainbows come in a variety of different sizes, but they are all rainbows. No single thing in these cases is black, the sky, or a rainbow. Humanity's propensity to generalize our definitions has often brought everything that is similar under the same explanation.

If we focus too much on our differences, then we become divided. At the same time, if we do not appreciate our uniqueness, then we lose our individuality. There has to be better alternatives to prejudice and conformity. Humanity has to do the work in finding a better path. The first step is realizing that things that are different and new are not inherently evil or a threat. We must stop homogenizing based off of generalizations and start recognizing and appreciating the gift of uniqueness. Let's stop judging by the outward appearance. Love is no thing, but countless expressions.

Prayer

Father God,

Help us to not be so close minded. The gates of our hearts are closed to the stranger. We perish because we are divided against ourselves. Nothing ever changes because we are afraid to be different and we punish those that are. Please, let our common love win over common hate. Show us the way Lord. We are not unwilling to learn but give us a hunger for wisdom. In You God, we do trust. Bless You for everything that You are and everything that You made us to be.

Amen.

"You blind Pharisee! First clean the inside of the cup and the plate, that the outside also may be clean." (Matthew 23:26 ESV)

A Clean Cup

There yet remains the option for a better future. Instead of being the victims of unwanted change, we must strive for progressive change and be the cause of it. Change is often imposed on us, but when we become the architects of the change we want to see, it is no longer oppressive. For too long humanity has underestimated its own power. Certainly, humanity has achieved great things. We have reached the stars, harnessed the power of lightning, and have found new ways to prolong human life. One would observe that humanity is always finding exciting solutions to difficult obstacles.

No matter how much we achieve, when we clean the outside of a cup, and the inside is dirty, there is no point in drinking from it. Humanity has the outer appearance of being an advanced civilization, but on the inside, we are always at war with ourselves. Has anyone ever asked the honest question, "If humanity is so advanced, then why aren't the people happy?" Certainly, the question has been asked before; so then, why has nothing changed? Have we become so advanced that children are bought and sold as property, there is a war every year, and some people would rather take their own life then keep on living?

We forgot the most important part of life: that each of us needs love to survive. Love is not for the few, and it is not for the most deserving; love gives to everyone without prejudice and at no cost. Without love, life is not worth living. The greatest miseducation of the world is that we put more value in what we can get for ourselves than in what we can give to others. A world in which everyone cares more about others than they do themselves is a world where no one is ever alone, forgotten, abused, or neglected. This is love, and it could be our greatest achievement or our greatest loss. It is a dream now, but so was putting a man on the moon.

Prayer

Loving Father,

We truly want to better ourselves, but we do not know how. So much effort is spent on making life easier, but not better. If there were magic words I could say, then I would say them, but no words I can say will make this world into what I want it to be. Only Your love can save us. Bless You Lord, for I know that Your love can accomplish all things. Show us the way we should take and let us not fail. Thank You Father.

Amen.

Wisdom of the Seasons

It has been a long journey. Life is a long journey with many seasons. In the Spring, we celebrate because we awaken to beauty. Mother's look into their children's eyes for the first time, Father's give away daughters to their husbands, the birds sing their songs, and the flowers put on their beautiful garments. Spring gives room to Summer, and in this season, we prepare. Farmers bear the heat and put their hands to work, the ant stores up food for a later use, families come together one last time before the seasons inhibit travel, and the animal's cross great distances to find pleasant habitation. Summer gives way to Fall, and in this season, the whole world braces itself for Winter. Trees shed their leaves, Grandmother's clean their homes, children go outside while they yet can, and Bears find suitable shelter for hibernation.

Winter, that final season, the harshest of them all, comes and tests us all. It is the final exam of the year. Those who studied will not be afraid, they will be confident, and they will be prepared for victory. Then, there are those who did not act wisely while they yet had the chance. The foolish did not prepare and took the seasons for granted. There were many signs that Winter was coming: the leaves did change their color, the birds did leave their homes, the farmers did put their crops in storage, and the reports did come that Winter was coming. Yet, in all their delights, the foolish did not consider that their delights, would eventually, end. Winter came, as we knew it would. The wise were given a crown of victory, and the foolish departed in their shame.

The meaning of this parable is this: Spring represents the years of our youth, which is new and full of wonder. Summer represents the years of our adulthood, which are the years in which we work to carve out a life for ourselves. Fall represents the years of old age, which is when we reflect and teach our children to act wisely. Winter is coming, and now is, in which the age comes to a close. There is no going back to the way things were before, for the end, is the begging of something else. How does one prepare with so little time? We must love wisdom with all that we have by honoring God, and by blessing our neighbors in word and deed.

Prayer

Our Father who is in heaven,

The end to our way of life must come and has come. There is no going back. Lead Your people into this new age. Winter is a hard time for us all, prepared or not, but teach us that it is better to be prepared. In Jesus name we pray, bless You Lord for all generations to come,

Amen.

Today's Gifts

Waiting with a friend far exceeds waiting alone. As much as a burden is easily lifted with many hands, how much easier is it to give a burden to God, than carry it alone? God is the friend we need when we find ourselves waiting. For when we draw near to God, anxiety is replaced with optimism, because all of God's plans are more excellent than our own. Alone one forgets who to wait on, and instead, we wait for. Be encouraged by a friend, and rather than search all day for the treasures of tomorrow, grab ahold of the gift that has already been given you. You have a relationship with the Divine.

Everything good comes in the proper time according to the will of God. We may know what we want, but God knows what is needed. So much time is wasted on what cannot be controlled. Staring at a clock won't make time pass by any faster, but you'd be amazed at how quickly time passes by when you are enjoying yourself. Relax and enjoy yourself in the presence of God. Seek that which feeds your soul. If you allow God to direct your life, then you will be satisfied in the end.

Time is a precious gift of the Lord that should not be wasted by worrying about the future. God has prepared the future, therefore, enjoy the day. Make good use of the day when you are able to do so, because it is often that you do not know what hasn't happened yet. If we focus on tomorrow's gifts, then we lose what is here and now. Today may offer us something far more desirable than what we were looking for. Because there is much we do not know, it is better to seek guidance from the One who knows exactly what to give us and when. Money can be a great gift, but if it were given to us too early, we would not know what to do with it. Why would a parent give their child a million dollars? Likewise, why would God give us something that we were not ready for?

Prayer

Blessed Creator,

We thank You for what You have already given us. Help us to enjoy the day and trust You for tomorrow. Teach us patience and how to celebrate early, because You never disappoint. Bless You always, now and forevermore.

Amen.

"Do not be deceived: God cannot be mocked. A man reaps what he sows. Whoever sows to please their flesh, from the flesh will reap destruction; whoever sows to please the Spirit, from the Spirit will reap eternal life." (Galatians 6:7-8 NIV)

From Famine to Feasting

Before he died, Paul the apostle, left us with this message: you reap what you sow. One cannot assume that humanity has learned this lesson; if it had, then the world would be a better place. How can an old farmer's saying be the very thing that can help make this world a better place? The answer is that it won't, not unless the people go beyond hearing the words, and take their hands to the plow and sow good seed.

Half-way through the 2020 the situation became extreme. An epic plague was ravaging our world. This new strain of Coronavirus forced us into isolation because it was no longer safe to go outside. As soon as we did, we saw that some of the very ones we look to for protection were the very ones robbing us of justice and destroying our lives. This was extreme. What followed, is that some of the people rose up and started destroying their own cities with fire. There was one extreme, then another, and another, and another, and so on.

When the authorities, which includes all models of leadership, sow into their members a chaotic set of circumstances, they will reap chaotic results. Conversely, if those same authorities sow love into their communities, the end result will be a community more loving to all. As we plant to the future, we must not expect to grow wheat if and when we find ourselves planting weeds. We must pull up the weeds, see them for what they are, and refuse to plant them any longer. Wisdom is the farmers wheat, and only it's seed will produce a future.

Prayer

Great Spirit, the maker of heaven and Earth,

You have prepared a table for us, and we have come to eat. Let us dine on wisdom and become wise. Feed us until we are full. We have been hungry for so long wanting wisdom. The fool's meal is not bread; it is not satisfying. Who will feed our children? We do not even have enough to feed ourselves. Bring us from famine to feasting for all generations to come. Thank You God for this food. Please, bless this food to the nourishment of our bodies.

Amen.

Wasting Away

John the apostle recorded that Lazarus of Bethany was ill, but to put it another way, he was dying. He was not suffering because of a lack of faith. He had the faith; not only that, but Jesus was actually a friend of the family. Lazarus called on his Lord, but His Lord allowed him to suffer until death. Have you called onto the Lord while everything was being taken from you?

Maybe you are like Lazarus. Ask yourself these questions: Am I dying? Am I defeated? Is my very soul torn into innumerable pieces? The reason why God is taking everything away from you is because God is setting you up to receive the treasures of His kingdom. He took everything away from the widow with the two mites so that she could be set up to give the last of what she had. The giving of the mites was an outward sign of what was happening inside. She was giving her heart to God. She couldn't give her best without giving her last.

God asked the widow at Zarephath to give the last meal she had for her and her son before they would die of hunger to Elijah. She had to give the last she had so that when God was ready to increase her, God would make much out of the little she had. By so doing, the woman would realize that the supply was not in what she could see, but in the unseen almighty God; the same God who called light out of darkness.

Long ago, Jesus told His followers, "Lazarus has died, and for your sake I am glad that I was not there, so that you may believe."

(John 11:14-15) What has to die in order for us to believe? It is when we have nothing that we learn the treasure we always have...is hope.

Prayer

Sometimes the crushing drives us crazy, but God. If it was not for the Lord, we would be without hope. In You God we find refuge. We had to lose everything to find You, even though we had You all along. Sometimes, we focus on what is seen when we need to stop looking and start seeing. Help us Lord to see You. How we desperately long to see You. You are invisible, but perceivable. Let us see with our hearts through heaven's eyes.

Amen.

Miracle of Hope

This is the story of my first, of many, miracles; a miracle that saved my life. It was my twenty fifth year in the fall of 2013 and I was staying with my aunt and uncle in the heart of Greenville, Texas. In the garage next to the house, memories of my elder brother's suicide were fresh but distant; fresh because it happened right next to where I was staying and distant because a few years had passed. At the time, I was in the house upstairs away from the garage. While sitting on the bed, something quite unexpected happened. I heard a voice coming from what appeared to be nothing. There wasn't supposed to be anyone home besides myself. But there it was loud, clear, and formless.

"It's me, God," explained the stranger. "I am God."

"What do you want with me?" I asked.

"It's time for you to come and be with me in heaven," insisted the stranger. Over and over again the voice repeated the words until I became dizzy. I heard the words which had no tone and no inflection to them. It was just a void with a message, and I believed it's suggestion.

"What must I do?" I asked aloud.

"Kill yourself. Kill yourself. Kill yourself and you will go to heaven," repeated the strange voice.

I sat on the bed disoriented for a time, until finally, I determined that I must obey God. That is when I got up off of the bed and found my cousin's gun fully loaded by the closet. I looked at the gun, the whole time hearing the voice beckon me to do what needed to be done. Then, I turned the safety off and went outside. Hiding behind the shed in the backyard, I sat with my hand on the trigger pointing the gun to my head hesitating.

> "Don't worry. It will just be a moment and you will be here with me," reassured the voice.

I put the gun down inhaling and exhaling slowly. Then, I picked the gun back up and pulled the trigger. Nothing happened. I checked the gun to see if I had done something wrong, but the gun had jammed or I had not cocked it properly. Confused, I thought, "If God wants me to kill myself, then I have to." So, I decided to overdose on pills instead and went back inside. In the house I climbed the steps and placed the gun in the pool room and considered that I could likely find pills in the kitchen.

Once there, I found a basket full of pill bottles atop of the fridge. I pulled out a random bottle of Aspirin, popped open the lid and…

> "Stop!" another voice, this time powerful and with authority commanding me. "That really was a devil, trying to kill you."

It was God, the real one, and I had been deceived like my brother had been years ago. My brother shot himself, but I, couldn't. Overwhelmed, I ran upstairs back to my room, fell on my knees, and cried to God:

"Save me!" over and over again shaken and in awe.

That was the day I'll never forget, the day God spoke to me, the day God stopped death, and the day I first believed in God.

Prayer

Almighty God,

I seek you during times of hopelessness.

I am low.

I trust Your abundant grace. I place my burdens under Your feet, Lord.

Give me rest and renew my strength. Give me the courage to face all that comes my way. The future is uncertain but I know that I will face it with You.

Father, be with me as I move forward through this mired path.

Amen.

Faith

For those who put their faith in God, all things are possible. Faith is trusting in, hoping in, and believing in something. It is like planting a seed. If you plant a seed in good soil, then it will grow. Conversely, if you plant a seed on a pile of rocks, then it will shrivel up and die. The love of God is good soil, but the riches of this world are merely stones by comparison. A woman will devote herself to what she has faith in, and just as her journey will follow the direction of her thoughts, she will rise or fall according to the quality of her meditations. When a woman cares for God, He cares for her. Conversely, when a woman cares for the world, it is the world which cares for her.

It is not wise to invest in a temporary thing, for once it has passed away, so too does the source of one's income go away. God is eternal and the flame of His love never diminishes over time. Conversely, this world represents a moment in time, for we cannot stay here forever. To follow God is to invest towards a guaranteed future while the world can only offer temporary pleasures. God made the world and all its pleasures; so then, do not measure the grain above the farmer. We trust that God can do anything, even raise the dead; therefore, our faith should be in the One who can guarantee us a good life.

Every tree was once a seed. Every achievement was once a dream. If a farmer neglects to water his seed, then he does not expect a harvest. Likewise, if a person does not feed their faith by continually seeking that which they hope for, then they will never find it. God never fails, and those who put their faith in Him are never disappointed. Therefore, those who have put their faith in God have planted their seeds assuredly.

Prayer

Dear God,

By our faith in You, we prosper. When we are attacked, our faith defends us. When we are hurt, by our faith You heal us. When we are brought low, faith lifts us up. Protect our faith. Never let the flame diminish but fan it until it is an all-consuming fire. We put our faith in You, and we know that You are true. Bless You now and forevermore.

Amen.

"He will wipe all tears from their eyes, and there will be no more death, suffering, crying, or pain. These things of the past are gone forever." (Revelation 21:4 CEV)

Death is Not the End

You will be reunited with your loved ones. Heaven promises everlasting joy for the departed, and it is a place where you will one day see all of your loved ones gathered together. There will be no more crying and no more pain. I have lost loved ones, and I have learned that no one wants to say goodbye. No one wants to live in a world where their loved ones are not in it. Losing a loved one is the hardest thing anyone will ever have to go through. Knowing that death is not the end, but a new beginning, makes everything that you are going through less impossible to deal with.

God is not punishing you, and their deaths are not your fault. No one is expecting you to act as though everything is okay, but remember, anyone who loves you wants you to be happy. That means that you do not have to stay bitter, angry, and miserable for your entire life. If you died, would you want that for your children? If not, then live! You are allowed to grieve in your own way and in your own time. We all want to live a happy life, and you can only do that if you try. There is no one who ever lived that did not face hard times. With age comes many experiences that we cannot avoid but hope never dies; hope is just hard to see sometimes.

Everyone has a time appointed to them when they meet God. We know that God lives, and that He prepares an eternal home for us in heaven. Your loved ones are happy where they are, so do not punish yourself for your loved one's blessing. The best thing you can do now is to honor your loved ones by taking care of yourself. When you do this, you are fulfilling the wishes of the ones who returned to God because they love you. You will get through this pain, you will find the strength, and you will live on never forgetting the ones you love.

Prayer

Our God who gives life,

We need You now to wrap us in Your arms. The pain makes it hard for us to even breath. Heal our hearts and help us. Have compassion on us and bring our souls out of the depths of despair. Give us strength. Help us to not be bitter or angry but to rejoice over Your children returning home. Please do this for us and bring Your children together again. We need You. Oh, how we need You. We do not understand Your will, but we desire to. In Jesus name we pray,

Amen.

Our God Lives!

When darkness falls and all hopes seem lost, praise our God because He lives! To some, God is a mother, to others a Father, and some do not define, but for all who hope in the Great Spirit our trust is the same. We trust that our God lives. He is life when there is death, light when there is darkness, and hope when there is despair. Let the people of God praise Him because it is better to be overcome with gladness over what He has done than to be overcome with the troubles of the world. There are more eulogies for the days we can never get back than there are praises for the days to come. Does it do us any good to live in regret?

We all fall down, but we are not meant to stay down. This is why we must encourage ourselves by celebrating the One who guarantees our prosperity. Praise makes the heart glad and edifies all those who see it. Far too many people have lost hope. They cannot bring themselves out of the pit of despair. It is not that they do not have the strength, but rather, they have lost the will. The praises of God give much hope and a will to those who have lost both. If God has ever done anything worthy of your gratitude, then praise Him. God did not help you then to forsake you now, and He will not leave a job half finished.

God saved you to prosper you. As the Psalmist says, "Give thanks to the Lord, for His love endures forever." Your end will not be bitter, but sweet, for His love towards you is eternal. The more troubles you have now will turn into greater gratitude later.

It is more often that we praise God for what our eyes have not yet seen than have. Therefore, expect good things, not because of your current circumstances, but because of God's loves towards you which promises a future worthy of praise.

Prayer

Praise You God,

Bless You, because You have never forsaken me. Even when I was faithless, You were faithful. Bless You Father because You are good and true. I do not despise You for troubles, but I bless You for the future You have promised me, a sweet end, and eternal life. Let our praises be heard all over the world and let Your people be encouraged because You live! In Jesus name we pray,

Amen.

About the Author

Jonathon McClellan is an award-winning author originally from Wichita, Kansas but now lives in Dallas, Texas. Coming from humble beginnings, he experienced poverty from an early age and realized that emotional poverty is perhaps the most crippling.

He first started writing devotionals for his local church at Cathedral of Hope as a way to work through his own early traumas from a difficult childhood. Since 2010, Jonathon has worked for various charities such as Save The Children, Children's International, the ACLU, the Human Rights Campaign and many more. Now, Jonathon works on feeding the soul as well as the body with powerful messages inspired by his battles with Schizophrenia, depression, and discrimination.

As time passed, Jonathon began questioning his own assumptions about who God loves, and came to the conclusion that a God of love would not exclude anyone at His table for being different. Today, he shares a message that God is radically inclusive. When Jonathon is not writing, he likes to spend his time singing, dancing, and being an activist.